מאמר
להבין ענין ראש חודש
תר"ס

FEMININE
FAITH

מאמר
להבין ענין ראש חודש
תר"ס

FEMININE
FAITH

a chasidic discourse by
Rabbi Shmuel Schneersohn
זצוקללה"ה נבג"מ זי"ע
of Lubavitch

•

translation and annotation by
Rabbi Shais Taub

additional annotation by
Rabbi Avraham D. Vaisfiche

KEHOT PUBLICATION SOCIETY
770 Eastern Parkway / Brooklyn, New York 11213

Feminine Faith

Published and Copyrighted © 2009
by
KEHOT PUBLICATION SOCIETY
770 Eastern Parkway / Brooklyn, New York 11213
(718) 774-4000 / Fax (718) 774-2718
editor@kehot.com

Orders:
291 Kingston Avenue / Brooklyn, New York 11213
(718) 778-0226 / Fax (718) 778-4148
www.kehot.com

ISBN: 978-0-8266-0749-2

Manufactured in the United States of America

CONTENTS

PREFACE

We are pleased to present *Feminine Faith*, an English rendition of a discourse by Rabbi Shmuel Schneersohn, fourth Lubavitcher Rebbe, as part of the acclaimed *Chasidic Herirage* Series.

Delivered on Shabbat Parshat Noach, Rosh Chodesh Marcheshvan, 5640, it examines the underlying idea behind the episode of the infamous Golden Calf, worshipped in the Sinai Desert. Having been exposed to the Egyptian view—which claimed that G-d is far too lofty to control creation, and thus relegated its sole management to the constellations, leaving Himself to play no role whatsoever in its management—the people felt justified in worshipping a calf, which they portrayed as a physical embodiment of the constellation of Aries.

The discourse explains why this was so erroneous, and confirming just the opposite to be true, that no one can challenge G-d's ability to alter the order of nature on earth. This is the fundamental Jewish belief and knowledge, which we received through Moses directly from the mouth of G-d.

The women, however, rejected Golden Calf, and as a special reward for their behavior, were given the holiday of Rosh Chodesh. Indeed, in the words of the author's grandson, Rabbi Yosef Yitzchak of Lubavitch, the discourse discusses "The holiday for women, the sin of the Golden Calf, and Pharaoh's mistake that G-d had abandoned creation to the hands of the angels and constellations."

*   *   *

It is important to note that as with many of the works of Rabbi Shmuel of Lubavitch, the present discourse, too, is founded upon discourses—of identical subject matter—that were originally delivered by Rabbi Schneur Zalman of Liadi, founder of the Chabad Movement, and Rabbi Menachem Mendel Schneersohn, third Lubavitcher Rebbe, author of "Tzemach Tedek." Furthermore, there exists an alternate version of the present discourse, in the form of transcriber's notes. All of these sources provide supplementary explanation of the sometimes obscure concepts of the subject matter, and were consulted for the annotations to the present volume.

The discourse was translated and annotated by Rabbi Shais Taub. Additional annotation was provided by Rabbi Avraham D. Vaisfiche. Special thanks are due to Rabbis Yosef B. Friedman and Dovid Olidort for their editorial guidance, and to Rabbi Mendel Laine for coordinating the project.

Kehot Publication Society

5 Tevet 5770
Brooklyn, New York

Facsimile of handwritten manuscript by Rabbi Shmuel Schneersohn

INTRODUCTION
AND SUMMARY

INTRODUCTION AND OVERVIEW

THE JEWISH WOMAN

Throughout the forty year sojourn of the Jewish people in the wilderness, the Jewish women repeatedly distinguished themselves as possessing a greater degree of spiritual sensitivity than the men. Two such incidents are given as reasons why the observance of Rosh Chodesh is considered to be a special time of celebration for women.

In describing the incident of the Golden Calf, the Torah states that Aaron said to them, *"Take the rings off the ears of your wives and children, and bring them to me." All the people took off their earrings and brought them to Aaron.*[1] The wording implies that the women refused to contribute towards this sinful cause and that the men then removed their own jewelry which they handed over to Aaron.[2]

Subsequently, regarding the construction of the Mishkan, the Torah specifically notes, *All the women whose hearts inspired them with wisdom spun the goats' wool.*[3] The commentators explain that since the women exhibited exceptional enthusiasm regarding this Heavenly work, they were granted the holiday of Rosh Chodesh when they are exempt from work.[4]

According to Kabbalah, it is the spiritual root of the female soul that accounts for the connection between the Jewish woman and the holiday of Rosh Chodesh.[5] In this light, the above mentioned episodes may be seen as but manifestations of a more essential feminine quality which is the focus of the discourse presented here.

Delivered by the fourth Lubavitcher Rebbe, Rabbi Shmuel Schneersohn, on Rosh Chodesh Cheshvan 5640, the

---

1. Exodus 32:2-3.

2. *Levush* 417:1. See also *Likkut Dinei Uminhagei Rosh Chodesh*, Ch. 3 (Kehot, 1990).

3. Exodus 35:26.

4. *Rosh* and *Daat Zekenim* on the verse ibid.

5. See Ch. 5 of the present discourse and fn. 102 there.

discourse examines the relationship between women and Rosh Chodesh and the unique quality of feminine spirituality, especially as this quality was evident in the women's refusal to participate in the Golden Calf. The feminine soul, Rabbi Shmuel explains, imbues women with a greater awareness of G-d's presence and, hence, a greater aversion to idolatry. As such, the discourse deals at length with the nature of idolatry, its essence and ideology as a way of understanding what predisposes women to reject the worship of false gods.

THE SECOND COMMANDMENT

The proscription against idol worship—*You shall have no other gods before Me* [6]—is the central prohibition of the Torah. Why does the verse make reference to "other gods," thereby seemingly acknowledging their existence but only prohibiting their worship? We find elsewhere in Scripture [7] that G-d is sometimes described as "G-d of the supernal beings," again seemingly supporting the notion that other deities do exist. Jewish faith rejects the very notion of a pantheon over which G-d but presides. Such an idea is not only inconsonant with Jewish belief but absolute anathema. How then are we to reconcile the complete rejection of the existence other gods with the Scripture's use of terminology which ostensibly recognizes their existence?

ORIGINS OF IDOLATRY

In his *Mishneh Torah*, [8] Maimonides describes the origins of idolatry. Tracing the history of religious experience back to the time of Adam, he outlines how polytheism was not originally devised in opposition to monotheism, but as a flawed attempt to better serve the one G-d by bestowing honor to the various forces of nature which G-d had set in place, particularly the constellations. By worshipping the forces of nature, early man actually believed he was showing honor to

---

6. Exodus 20:3; Deuteronomy 5:7.   136:2; Daniel 2:47 and 11:36.

7. Ibid. 10:17; Joshua 22:22; Psalms   8. Laws of Idolatry 1:1.

their Maker. Over the course of time, this already mistaken theology devolved into outright deification of these forces— their worshippers accrediting independent power to them.

It is undeniable that there are forces at work in the universe. However, these powers are in no way autonomous or ontologically independent. They are all just "like an axe in the hands of the woodchopper"[9] who uses them according to his whim. The grave error of the original idolaters was not in recognizing that the flow of creative energy enters this world by passing through various channels, but in fallaciously attributing self-governance to these agents which they accordingly sought to appease through worship.

ASTROLOGICAL INFLUENCES AND MINISTERING ANGELS

The Talmudic term for idolatry is "worship of the stars and constellations,"[10] for, as alluded to above, the original polytheism was based on a belief in the influences of the constellations. Astrology, however, is not inherently idolatrous;[11] far from it.[12] The constellations are understood to represent channels for the creative energy as it passes from the spiritual realms and into the physical plane. The heavenly counterparts to the constellations are the ministering angels who also function to transmit this energy "downward" to the physical universe. In either case, they are but conduits for the flow of a power that is not their own. It is the false attribution of independent will or power to these conduits that constitutes idolatry.

9. *Moreh Nevuchim* III, Ch. 29; *Zohar* I:31:1; Isaiah 10:15.

10. *Avodat kochavim u'mazalot* in Hebrew (often abbreviated to *akum*).

11. For instance, we find that Abraham, the father of monotheistic belief, practiced astrology, only G-d told him to ignore its signs because he would be immune to them. See Genesis 15:5 and *Rashi* there, based on *Nedarim* 32a and *Bereshit Rabbah* 44:10. Also see *Shabbat* 156a-b which describes the basic legitimacy of reading astrological signs, but that through service of G-d, one may circumvent such influences and should pay them no mind.

12. Just as, let us say, acknowledging the effects of the gravitational or electromagnetic forces.

Thus, when speaking of "other gods," the Torah refers to entities that may actually exist—whether physically or spiritually—and to which people may erroneously attribute independent power. However, these objects of deification are in truth no more than mere created beings that are subservient to and, moreover, utterly dependent upon G-d. It is only that since they function in the position of intermediaries[13] that they are mistakenly deemed worthy of honor or worship.

DETAILED PROVIDENCE

(The discourse contrasts the Jewish belief with idolatrous theology, particularly as adhered to by the Egyptians at the time of the Exodus.) The lure of idolatry which enticed the non-Jewish world of that time was that it seemed to address the fear that G-d is far too lofty and remote to deal directly with earthly events. Since, from the idolatrous perspective, G-d could not possibly be relied upon to involve Himself with the physical plane, one could turn to his "delegates"—the constellations and ministering angels.

The fallacy lies not only in the fact that these agents are powerless, but that they do not interrupt G-d's directorship of worldly affairs. G-d may work through these channels but they a) are possessed of no will of their own and b) do not constitute separate entities from G-d but rather, like all created beings, have no independent existence unto themselves. Thus, it is none other than G-d, and G-d alone, who brings about all events with specific providence for every detail.

---

13. Even in this regard they are not deemed "indispensable intermediaries" that must be reckoned with in order to relate to G-d.

While according to some *halachic* opinions the worship of G-d through an intermediary—known as *sheetuf*, lit., "partnership"—may not violate the prohibition of idolatry as required of non-Jews by the Seven Noachide Laws, it is without question strictly forbidden to Jews. (*Rama, Orach Chaim* 156 and *Darkei Moshe*, ad loc; see also *Bechorot* 2b, *Tosfot* s.v. *Shemah*; *Sanhedrin* 63b, *Tosfot* s.v. *Asur*; *Ran* on *Avoda Zara*, end Ch. 1. See, however, *Likkutei Sichot*, vol. 25, p. 192.)

IMMANENCE AND TRANSCENDENCE

While G-d exists utterly independent from and irrespective to creation,[14] He is also involved intimately with the affairs of this world. G-d is at once both immanent and transcendent, pervading all of creation and also inherently removed from it. Here we find the true answer to the apparent difficulty which the idolatrous position seeks to address through the deification of the constellations and ministering angels. If G-d is immanently present, then reliance upon intermediaries is completely unnecessary, for one may turn directly to G-d for any concern. Accordingly, the greater the individual's awareness of G-d's immanence, the less susceptible he or she will be to the case for idolatry.

The discourse which follows explains that the sensitivity to the immanent presence of G-d is more natural for women than for men; hence, they are more likely to utterly reject the argument for the worship of intermediaries. The reason that women have a greater intuitive understanding of the immanent aspect of G-d is due to the spiritual source of the souls which derives from a different plane than that of men.

MASCULINE AND FEMININE SPIRITUAL MODALITIES

The spiritual worlds are organized into a system of ten modalities or distinct emanations of G-dliness called *sefirot*. Each modality, or group thereof,[15] constitutes a plane of functionality within that world. The group of *sefirot* known as *z'eyr anpin* (or *z'a*)[16] is comprised of the six emotional *sefirot* whose function is to imbue various "colors" of creative energy necessary to generate the creation of a subsequent world. This energy, however, must pass through the lower plane com-

---

14. To regard G-d merely as Creator is inaccurate, for He exists utterly independent from and unaffected by the creation. Creation is merely a relationship or a context for perceiving G-d, but certainly does not describe G-d's Essence.

15. Referred to as a *partzuf* (lit., "profile"), this is a *sefirah* or group of *sefirot* which constitute a specific phase in the devolvement of creative energy through any given world.

16. See fn. 105 on the discourse.

prised of the *sefirah* of *malchut*[17] alone. It is in *malchut* that
the energy of *z'a* is deposited and nurtured so that through
the elaborative effect of *malchut*, this energy may emerge fully
articulated as a world unto its own. This progenitive partnership between *z'a* and *malchut* is the archetype for biological
conception and birth and indeed, each one is the model for
masculinity and femininity respectively.

From the perspective of *z'a*, the creation of a subsequent
world is buffered by its relationship with *malchut*. *Z'a* does
not directly relate to lower planes but instead gives its energy
to *malchut* wherein it may gestate. *Z'a* thus remains aloof
from the ensuing creation which it has fathered while *malchut*
is directly involved with the new plane of existence. The par-
allels to biological paternity and motherhood are obvious and
intended.

SOULS OF Z'A AND SOULS OF MALCHUT

Because the souls of women derive from *malchut*, they are
aware of how G-dly energy engenders new creations. Men, on
the other hand, whose souls are from *z'a*, tend to share its
obliviousness to this process. Their conception of G-d is generally characterized by an appreciation for His creative power
but not how that translates into actual creation. As such, it
may be said, that a woman is aware of how G-d brings this
world into being while a man regards G-d's role (as typified by
the function of *z'a*) as sublime and aloof.

Hence, men may find it more difficult to sense G-d's detailed providence while women more readily appreciate that it
is G-d Himself who directly controls all earthly affairs. It is
this perspective that immunes women from the proclivity to
seek out more tangible or immediate objects of worship and
allows them to feel G-d's immediate presence even in the lowest realms of creation.

SIN OF THE GOLDEN CALF

In light of the above, it may be understood why women as a

---

17. See fn. 102 on the discourse.

group did not participate in the sin of the Golden Calf.[18] After the plagues and miraculous exodus had shown the futility of the Egyptian deity, namely the constellation of Aries,[19] there were those[20] who believed that this was merely a sign that its neighboring constellation, Taurus, had defeated it and taken control. Thus, when Moses was thought to have delayed from returning from the mountaintop, the idolaters who had joined the Israelites in the desert[20] convinced many of them to worship Taurus, the bull, by constructing a golden calf. The women, however, were not taken in by this argument as it was obvious to them that the downfall of Egypt was brought about directly by G-d.

ROSH CHODESH AND WOMEN

As reward[21] for not participating in this sin, Jewish women were given the holiday of Rosh Chodesh, the day on which the new moon appears,[22] as a special time of celebration.[23] The moon, like women, is an embodiment of *malchut*.[24] Just as *malchut* receives its energy from *z'a* which it then passes on to lower realms, the moon receives its light from the sun which it then reflects to the earth.

Because it is their connection to *malchut* that makes women sensitive to G-d's role in earthly events and thus prevented them from accepting the arguments for the worship of the golden calf, it is fitting that women be given the privilege of uniquely observing the holiday of Rosh Chodesh.

---

18. *Levush* 417:1. See also *Likkut Dinei Uminhagei Rosh Chodesh*, Ch. 3 (Kehot, 1990).

19. See Chapter Four of the discourse.

20. Namely, the "mixed multitude" mentioned in Exodus 12:38. See fn. 15 on the discourse.

21. See fn. 4 on the discourse.

22. The first day of the new month in the Jewish calendar is the day on which the new moon appears after having fully waned.

23. Jewish law states that it is customary for women to refrain from work on Rosh Chodesh (*Shulchan Aruch, Orach Chaim* 417:1). The custom may vary from place to place regarding which labors women may or may not perform (*Rama*). One commentary (*Shaarei Teshuvah*) mentions that men who make a point not to do work on *Rosh Chodesh* are merely ignorant.

24. See fns. 115-117 on the discourse.

NOTE ON THE HEBREW TEXT: In vowelizing the Hebrew words in this edition we have followed the grammatical rules of the Holy Tongue, which occasionally differ from the traditional or colloquial pronunciation. The original footnotes by the publisher of the Hebrew text appear at the end of the *maamar*.

TRANSLATION
AND
COMMENTARY

B.H.

Shabbat, Rosh Chodesh Marcheshvan. Noach

A HOLIDAY FOR WOMEN

[We shall attempt] to understand the concept of Rosh Chodesh, literally, the "head of the month." Just as the head contains the overall vitality [of the body],[1] the "head" of the month contains the overall vitality of the entire month.[2]

[Similarly,] just as Rosh Hashanah contains the overall vitality for the entire [coming] year,[3] Rosh Chodesh contains the overall vitality for the ensuing month, encompassing the vitality of the next thirty days. This entire concept needs to be [better] understood.

In addition, we need to understand why Rosh Chodesh is considered a special holiday for women,[4] who observe it more carefully than do men.[5]

The reason for this is that they [the women] did not agree to hand over their jewelry to their husbands for the making of the Golden Calf;[6] in this merit, the Holy One Blessed be He rewarded them with Rosh Chodesh as a day to observe more carefully than men.

This seems to contradict [the *halachic* principle] that women are exempt from [performing] time-based positive commandments;[7] since Rosh Chodesh is a time-based com-

---

1. See *Tanya*, Ch. 51. Although the soul's influence as a vitalizing force is felt in all parts of the body, its powers are centralized in the brain, the nerve center which regulates and sends commands to all other organs. Similarly, Rosh Chodesh is the "nerve center" of each month from whence all of the vitality for that month is apportioned to all of its other days.

2. See *Shefa Tal* 8:3 (*Tal Kama*, 72); *Likkutei Torah, Rosh Hashanah* 58a ff.; *Maamarei Admur Hazaken, 5567,* p. 53; *Ateret Rosh*, 3b; *Or Hatorah, Korach*, p. 689.

In a transcriber's notes of the discourse: "The reason for the term 'Rosh Chodesh' is because it is the head of the entire month. A human head comprises the entire body, while all the limbs are the particulars. Similarly, Rosh Chodesh comprises one entire month, while all the days of the month are the particulars. And Rosh Hashanah, which translates literally as 'the head of the year,' comprises the entire ensuing year."

ב״ה, שר״ח מ״ח נח

לְהָבִין עִנְיַן רֹאשׁ חֹדֶשׁ*, שֶׁנִּקְרָא רֹאשׁ חֹדֶשׁ שֶׁכְּמוֹ הָרֹאשׁ הוּא כְּלָלִיּוּת חַיּוּת הָאָדָם, כֵּן רֹאשׁ הַחֹדֶשׁ הוּא הַכּוֹלֵל כְּלָלִיּוּת הַחַיּוּת² שֶׁל כָּל הַחֹדֶשׁ כּוּלוֹ,

וּכְמוֹ רֹאשׁ הַשָּׁנָה הוּא כְּלָלִיּוּת חַיּוּת³ כָּל הַשָּׁנָה, כֵּן רֹאשׁ חֹדֶשׁ הוּא כְּלָלִיּוּת חַיּוּת כָּל הַחֹדֶשׁ, שֶׁכּוֹלֵל חַיּוּת כְּלָלִיּוּת שֶׁל שְׁלֹשִׁים יוֹם, וְצָרִיךְ לְהָבִין עִנְיָנוּ,

וְגַם צָרִיךְ לְהָבִין מִפְּנֵי מָה רֹאשׁ חֹדֶשׁ הוּא יוֹם טוֹב שֶׁל נָשִׁים⁴ שֶׁמְּשַׁמְּרוֹת אוֹתוֹ יוֹתֵר מֵהָאֲנָשִׁים⁵,

וְהוּא מִפְּנֵי שֶׁלֹּא רָצוּ לִיתֵּן אֶת נִזְמֵיהֶן לְבַעֲלֵיהֶן בְּמַעֲשֵׂה הָעֵגֶל, וּבִשְׂכַר זֶה נָתַן הַקָּדוֹשׁ בָּרוּךְ הוּא שְׂכָרָן שֶׁיִּהְיוּ מְשַׁמְּרוֹת רֹאשׁ חֹדֶשׁ יוֹתֵר מֵאֲנָשִׁים,

אֲשֶׁר לִכְאוֹרָה זֶהוּ נֶגֶד מַה שֶׁהַנָּשִׁים פְּטוּרִים מִמִּצְוַת עֲשֵׂה שֶׁהַזְּמַן גְּרָמָא⁷, וְרֹאשׁ חֹדֶשׁ הוּא הַתָּלוּי בִּזְמַן, וּמִפְּנֵי מָה

---

3. See *Likkutei Torah, Tavo* 41c; ibid., *Rosh Hashanah* 53d and 58a; *Ateret Rosh*, ibid. See also *Kuntres UMaayan*, Discourses Eighteen & Nineteen (in English (Kehot, 2006): *Overcoming Folly*, p. 258 ff.).

4. See Jerusalem Talmud, *Pesachim*, beg. Ch. 4; *Pirkei d'Rabbi Eliezer* Ch. 45, and *Radal* there.; *Rashi* on *Megillah* 22b, s.v. *Roshei Chadashim; Or Hatorah, Chanukah*, vol. 5, p. 1864; sources cited in *Likkutei Sichot*, vol. 8, p. 315, fn. 8.

5. See *Likkutei Torah, Berachah* 97b ff.; *Or Hatorah, Bereshit*, p. 24; commentary of *Radak* on I Samuel 20:19; *Likkutei Sichot*, vol. 3, p. 862, fn. 49.

6. *Levush* 417:1. See also *Likkut Dinei Uminhagei Rosh Chodesh*, Ch. 3 (Kehot, 1990).

7. See *Kiddushin* 29a. See also *Torat Shmuel—Sefer 5638*, p. 158 ff. and sources cited there. Women are generally relieved of any positive mitzvah that must be performed at a specific time, for instance, reciting the *Shema* in the morning and at night or wearing a *tallit* or *tefillin* in the daytime.

In a transcriber's notes of the discourse: "There are many reasons for

mandment, why should women, who are generally relieved of such time-based obligations, be *more* careful in observing it than men who are obligated in all time-based matters?

(As for the fact that the new moon used to be sanctified according to the testimony of witnesses rather than according to astronomic calculation:[8] We are familiar with the statement in the Mishnah[9] that the determination of the new moon was also based upon calculation; the testimony of witnesses who had actually *seen* the *molad*[10] was necessary [only as confirmation]. Furthermore, in our day,[11] when the new moon is *not* established by testimony of witnesses, we depend *solely* upon calculation. As such, Rosh Chodesh is indeed a time-based commandment.[12])

INCOMPREHENSIBILITY OF THE SIN OF THE GOLDEN CALF

We will presently [be able to] understand all of this by first explaining the underlying idea behind the episode of the Golden Calf. Upon seeing *that Moses delayed in descending from the mountaintop*,[13] and that the sixth [hour][14] had arrived

---

this. One is, for restrained by time, a woman is duty-bound to her husband. And we do find that women are exempt from some of the great *mitzvot*, such as *shofar*, *sukkah*, or *lulav*. Rosh Chodesh, too, is specifically time-bound, because a day earlier and a day later are not related to 'Rosh Chodesh.' Now, although the prohibition of working on Rosh Chodesh is only a custom, nevertheless, it is a legitimate custom, as stated in *Pirkei d'Rabbi Eliezer* and in the Jerusalem Talmud, and so why was it given specifically to women? *Pirkei d'Rabbi Eliezer* records the following reason: When the mixed multitude misled the Jewish people to create the Golden Calf, and then announced, 'Remove the golden rings,' the women refused, and so were rewarded

with the holiday of Rosh Chodesh. But why is specifically Rosh Chodesh the reward for refusing to participate in the Calf?"

8. This statement refutes an unspoken attempt to answer the question as to why women are more stringent in their observance of Rosh Chodesh. If one should assert that Rosh Chodesh is actually *not* a time-based commandment because its induction is not automatically triggered by the passage of time but rather proclaimed by the High Court based on eyewitness testimony, then the following explanation will dismiss such an argument.

9. Rosh Hashanah 2:6 ff; *Bartenura* and *Tosfot Yom Tov* there.

יִהְיוּ הַנָּשִׁים שֶׁפְּטוּרִים מִדָּבָר הַתָּלוּי בִּזְמַן יִהְיוּ מְשַׁמְּרוֹת
רֹאשׁ חֹדֶשׁ הַתָּלוּי בִּזְמַן יוֹתֵר מֵאֲנָשִׁים שֶׁחַיָּיבִים בְּכָל דָּבָר
הַתָּלוּי בִּזְמַן?

(וּמַה שֶׁהָיוּ מְקַדְּשִׁים עַל פִּי הָרְאִיָּה וְלֹא תָלוּי בִּזְמַן,
הֲלֹא יָדוּעַ מִמַּה שֶׁכָּתוּב בַּמִּשְׁנָה שֶׁהָיָה גַם עַל פִּי חֶשְׁבּוֹן, רַק
שֶׁהָיוּ צְרִיכִים לָבוֹא עֵדִים שֶׁרָאוּ מוֹלַד הַלְּבָנָה, וְגַם עַכְשָׁיו
שֶׁאֵין מְקַדְּשִׁים עַל פִּי הָרְאִיָּה, בֶּאֱמֶת מְכֻוָּנִים עַל פִּי חֶשְׁבּוֹן[י]
לְבַד גַּם כֵּן, וְאִם כֵּן הוּא תָלוּי בִּזְמַן כו׳).

וְיוּבַן בְּהֶקְדֵּם כְּלָלִיּוּת עִנְיָן מַעֲשֵׂה הָעֵגֶל, שֶׁאָמְרוּ הָעֵרֶב
רַב לְיִשְׂרָאֵל בִּרְאוֹתָם כִּי בֹשֵׁשׁ מֹשֶׁה[ס] לָרֶדֶת מִן הָהָר, וְכִי

---

10. Lit., "birth" of the new moon. See the aforementioned *Likkut Dinei Uminhagei Rosh Chodesh*, Ch. 1, law 4.

11. Upon disbanding the *Sanhedrin* in the 4th century CE, Hillel II established a fixed calendar. The lengths of the months are thus predetermined based on astronomic calculations rather than depending upon actual testimony that the new moon has appeared. See *Likkutei Sichot*, vol. 16, p. 94, fn. 10.

12. Thus, the question remains: being that the occurrence of Rosh Chodesh is pre-scheduled, its observance is an entirely time-based commandment from which women seemingly should be exempted altogether.

13. Exodus 32:1. The day after the nation heard the Ten Commandments at Sinai, Moses ascended to the mountain to receive the written tab-

lets. Moses informed the people that he would return on the sixth hour of the fortieth day from his leaving. Being, however, that in the Jewish calendar, the new day begins at nightfall and Moses left in the morning, the day of his departure was an incomplete day and not to have been reckoned as the first of his forty-day absence (*Rashi* on this verse, and on *Shabbat* 89a).

14. Noontime of what was incorrectly reckoned to be the fortieth day, the appointed time for Moses' return. In the verse (ibid.), the Hebrew word for "delayed" is "*boshesh*" (בשש). The Talmud (*Shabbat* 89a) homiletically interprets this as one of the Satan's claims: "*Ba'u shesh*" (באו שש), "the sixth hour has arrived"—this was the hour that Moses had designated as his return time, but since there was no sign of him, Moses was not going to return.

and [Moses] had not returned, the mixed multitude[15] convinced the Jews to make the calf. The Satan's wily plan succeeded and they proclaimed, *Here is your god, O Israel, who
took you out of Egypt.*[16]

This is most astounding, especially considering that this
was a "Generation of Knowledge."[17] How could they think
that a Golden Calf made of inert matter was a god and the
one who had taken them out of Egypt?[18]

[Their own] experience should have refuted [such a no-
tion]: they all saw that no such calf existed at the time of the
Exodus from Egypt, and indeed, were Moses to have come
[on time], the mixed multitude would never have been able to
entice them into making the calf in the first place. It was only
due to their error and the [fact that it was a] cloudy day,[19]
which led them into making that he was late, that the mixed
multitude even had the opportunity to entice the Jews. Nor
would the Satan's wily plan [to have them form the calf] have
succeeded [without that opportunity]. The entire notion, as
well as what this had to do with the fact that they thought
that Moses was late, remains totally incomprehensible.

---

15. EREV RAV, in the Hebrew. This
term refers to a group of Egyptian
and other non-Jewish residents of
Egypt who, during the time of the
Exodus, attached themselves to the Israelites in the wake of the Ten
Plagues. See Exodus 12:38 and commentaries there.

16. Exodus 32:4, 8.

17. GENERATION OF KNOWLEDGE. *Dor
De'ah*, in the Hebrew. A special title
reserved in rabbinic literature to describe the generation that witnessed

the revelation at Sinai and that stud-
ied Torah directly from Moses. See
Zohar II:62b; *Pri Eitz Chaim, Shaar
Chag Hamatzot*, Ch. 1; *Maamarei Admur HaEmtza'ee, Devarim*, vol. 1, p.
76, where it is referenced further.

18. In a transcriber's notes of the discourse: "The Calf was made out of
molten gold. Anyone with any ink-
ling of knowledge understands that it
is impossible to say *Here is your god*
regarding metal or molten gold!
…How did they exchange G-d for a
calf made of gold and proclaim that it

בָּא שֵׁשׁ וְלֹא בָא, שֶׁיַעֲשׂוּ הָעֵגֶל וְהִצְלִיחַ מַעֲשֵׂה שָׂטָן וְאָמְרוּ אֵלֶּה אֱלֹקֶיךָ יִשְׂרָאֵל אֲשֶׁר הֶעֱלוּךָ מֵאֶרֶץ מִצְרָיִם,

שֶׁזֶּהוּ בֶּאֱמֶת פִּלְאֵי פְלָאוֹת וְכָל שֶׁכֵּן עַל דּוֹר דֵּיעָה[יא] שֶׁיַּחְשְׁבוּ כֵן, שֶׁעֵגֶל זָהָב עָשׂוּי מְדּוּמָם גַּשְׁמִי יִהְיֶה הוּא הָאֱלֹקָה, וְהוּא אֲשֶׁר הוֹצִיא אֶת יִשְׂרָאֵל מִמִּצְרַיִם,

שֶׁהַחוּשׁ מַכְחִישׁוֹ שֶׁכּוּלָם רָאוּ שֶׁלֹּא הָיָה עֵגֶל בְּעֵת צֵאתָם מִמִּצְרַיִם, וְאִם הָיָה מֹשֶׁה בָּא תְּחִלָּה לֹא הָיָה מָקוֹם כְּלָל לְעֶרֶב רַב לֵאמֹר לְיִשְׂרָאֵל וּלְפַתּוֹתָם עַל מַעֲשֵׂה הָעֵגֶל, רַק מִפְּנֵי טָעוּתָם וְיוֹם הַמְעוּנָן[יב] אֲשֶׁר לְפִי דַעְתָּם אִיחַר זְמַנּוֹ, אָז הָיָה מָקוֹם לְעֶרֶב רַב לְפַתּוֹתָם וְהִצְלִיחַ מַעֲשֵׂה שָׂטָן כו׳ שֶׁעָשׂוּ כו׳. אַךְ לִכְאוֹרָה אֵינוֹ מוּבָן לְעֵינֵינוּ כְּלָל, וְשַׁיָּיכוּתוֹ לְעִנְיַן מַה שֶׁאִיחַר מֹשֶׁה לָבוֹא לְפִי דַעְתָּם כו׳.

---

took them out of Egypt?"

19. See *Rashi* on Exodus 32:1 (and on *Shabbat* 89a): "It is impossible to conclude that they erred because the day was cloudy, and the people's mistake was whether noontime had arrived yet or not—which was the hour that Moses had designated for his return—for Moses didn't actually return until the following day." I.e., they erred in their calculation of the number of days, not in the number of hours.

From *Rashi's* words, however, it's evident that there is an opinion which maintains that their error was regarding the time of "six hours into the day." But as far as the discussion in the discourse, the prevailing opinion of what actually occurred is irrelevant. Apparently, the discourse points out that the fact that there is even such an opinion—that their entire error was regarding the time of noon—only serves to strengthen the incomprehension of the episode of the Golden Calf: Was it just because of such a simple error that they would resort to idolatry?!

2.

THE THEOLOGICAL ARGUMENT FOR IDOLATRY

The matter [may be understood as follows]: The critical [the-ological] error made by Pharaoh, King of Egypt,[20] who said, *Who is the L-rd that I should listen to Him?...I know not the L-rd,*[21] and therefore *I will not release the Israelites*[22]—an error shared in common with all of the other deniers of the [true] faith—is *not* that they actually reject the existence of G-d.[23] All [idolaters] know Him, that He is the Creator of all Crea-tions, and that He is Eternal, as the verse states, *From the ris-ing of the sun to its setting, My name will be great among the na-tions, and in every place incense will be offered to My name.*[24] Indeed, as the Sages say, [even the idolaters] call Him "G-d of gods,"[25] as in the verse, *Praise the G-d of the supernal beings.*[26]

Rather, their error lies in maintaining that *G-d has aban-doned the world,*[27] relinquishing [responsibility] for its man-agement to the constellations[28] and ministering angels,[29] and empowering them to run the world according to their wish and whim. Furthermore, [they maintain that] He Himself plays no part whatsoever in managing [the world], being that He is exalted and elevated beyond such physical phenomena as transpire on earth, and that it would be degrading for Him to lower Himself to [attend to] such lowly matters here below. For this reason, He has "abandoned" their management to the ministering angels and constellations.

This is what is meant by the verse,[30] *The heavens are the L-rd's heavens, but the earth He gave to the children of man.*[31] The term "heavens" [here] does not refer to the physical heav-

---

20. See *Sefer Ha'arachim—Chabad*, vol. 2, s.v. *Ummot Ha'olam*, p. 277 ff.

21. Exodus 5:2.

22. Ibid.

23. This statement is obvious hyper-bole. The point is that, in principle, it is not a lack of belief in G-d that prompts idolaters to worship con-stellations and other forces. It is their inability to conceive of G-d as being directly involved in worldly events, as the discourse continues to explain.

24. Malachi 1:11. See *Rashi, Radak*, and *Metzudat David* on this verse.

25. *Menachot* 110a. See footnote in

ב.

וְהָעִנְיָן הוּא כִּי הִנֵּה עִיקַר טָעוּת פַּרְעֹה[כג] מֶלֶךְ מִצְרַיִם שֶׁאָמַר מִי הוי' אֲשֶׁר אֶשְׁמַע בְּקוֹלוֹ, לֹא יָדַעְתִּי אֶת הוי''[כד], אֲשֶׁר עַל כֵּן לֹא אֲשַׁלַּח אֶת יִשְׂרָאֵל, וְעַל דֶּרֶךְ זֶה גַּם שְׁאָרֵי הַכּוֹפְרִים בֶּאֱמוּנָה כוּ', אֵין הָעִנְיָן שֶׁמַּכְחִישִׁים בַּאֲמִיתִיוּת הַמָּצְאוֹ מַמָּשׁ, כִּי כּוּלָם יוֹדְעִים אוֹתוֹ, שֶׁהוּא יוֹצֵר כָּל הַיְצוּרִים וְהוּא נִצְחִי, וּכְמוֹ שֶׁכָּתוּב כִּי מִמִּזְרַח שֶׁמֶשׁ עַד מְבוֹאוֹ[כה] גָּדוֹל שְׁמִי בַּגּוֹיִם וּבְכָל מָקוֹם מוּקְטָר כוּ' וּכְמַאֲמַר רַזַ"ל דְּקָרוּ לֵיהּ אֱלָקָא דֶאֱלָקַיָּיא[כו], וּכְדִכְתִיב הוֹדוּ לֵאלֹקֵי הָאֱלֹקִים[כז],

אֶלָּא שֶׁעִנְיַן טָעוּתָם שֶׁהוּא[כח]* שֶׁאוֹמְרִים עָזַב ה' אֶת הָאָרֶץ[כח] בְּיַד הַמַּזָּלוֹת וְשָׂרִים הָעֶלְיוֹנִים, וְנָתַן לָהֶם הַכֹּחַ שֶׁיִּהְיוּ הֵם הַמַּנְהִיגִים אֶת הָאָרֶץ כְּפִי רְצוֹנָם וְאַוַּת נַפְשָׁם, וְאֵין לוֹ יִתְבָּרֵךְ שׁוּם חֵלֶק בְּהַהַנְהָגָה כְּלָל, לִהְיוֹת כִּי הוּא מְרוֹמָם וְנַעֲלֶה מֵעֶרֶךְ הַהַגְשָׁמָה הַנַּעֲשֶׂה עַל פְּנֵי הָאֲדָמָה, וַהֲרֵי הוּא הַשְׁפָּלָה לְפָנָיו יִתְבָּרֵךְ לְהַשְׁפִּיל אֶת עַצְמוֹ בַּעֲלוּלִים הַשְׁפֵלִים שֶׁלְּמַטָּה, וְלָכֵן עָזַב אוֹתָם בִּידֵי הַשָּׂרִים וְהַמַּזָּלוֹת שֶׁהֵם יִנְהֲגוּ אוֹתָם,

וְזֶהוּ שֶׁאָמַר הַכָּתוּב הַשָּׁמַיִם שָׁמַיִם לַהוי'[כט] וְהָאָרֶץ נָתַן לִבְנֵי אָדָם, פֵּירוּשׁ הַשָּׁמַיִם אֵין כַּוָּנָתוֹ עַל הַשָּׁמַיִם הַגַּשְׁמִים,

---

Torat Shmuel—Sefer 5632, vol. 1, p. 53.

26. Psalms 136:2.

27. Ezekiel 8:12; 9:9.

28. MAZALOT, in Hebrew, having the same etymology as *nozel*, to flow. The constellations are conduits for the flow of creative energy between the spiritual and physical realms. Hence,

this flow may be erroneously attributed to the *mazal* itself.

29. The ministering angels, like the *mazalot*, function to regulate the flow of energy into this plane of creation.

30. In *Maamarei Admur Hazaken, Inyanim*, p. 385: "Their error is derived from the following verse."

31. Psalms 115:16.

ens but rather [to their spiritual parallel] as in *the sublime heavens.*[32] Similarly, [the verse] *For as high as the heaven is above the earth*[33] describes the qualitative distance between the spiritual and physical planes: Just as the physical heavens seem to the naked eye as exalted and removed from the earth, which is the lowest thing, likewise, all of the spiritual entities such as the angels and the spiritual worlds of *Beriah, Yetzirah* and *Asiyah*[34] are *the L-rd's*, who conducts them with "detailed supervision."[35]

In contrast, due to *the earth and all that is upon it*[36] being the lowest creations, it would be degrading for Him to pay attention to them with detailed supervision. Therefore,[37] He has empowered the constellations and ministering angels to manage and supervise such affairs according to their wish and whim by the power with which He has invested them, namely, to supervise with detailed supervision all of the specific details attendant to the mundane phenomena that occur upon the physical earth below.

G-D BY PROXY: THE CONSTELLATIONS AND MINISTERING ANGELS

This is the meaning of *but the earth He gave to the children of*

---

32. Proverbs 25:3. The idolaters' perception is that G-d concerns Himself only with the happenings of the spiritual planes and not with terrestrial affairs. The discourse continues elaborating in detail on this erroneous idea until the end of this chapter.

33. Psalms 103:11.

34. THE SPIRITUAL WORLDS. Kabbalah and Chasidus explain the phenomenon of the creation of a finite physical universe by an Infinite Creator with the concept of *tzimtzum*—contraction and concealment. G-d effected a series of concealments of His presence and infinitude, resulting ultimately in the creation of our physical universe, through a virtually total concealment of G-d. The non-corporeal intermediate steps between the Creator and this material world are called "Worlds," referring to the basic levels of spiritual existence in the creative process. The differentiation reflects their level of concealment of the divine light, the higher worlds receiving in a more revealed form.

In general, there are Four Worlds: *Atzilut* (World of Emanation, a state of proximity and relative unity with G-d); *Beriah* (World of Creation); *Yetzirah* (World of Formation); *Asiyah* (World of Action or Making, the final stage in the creative process). The four worlds have been compared to the elements inherent to building a

כִּי אִם עַל דֶּרֶךְ כְּמוֹ שָׁמַיִם לָרוּם⁵ וּכְמוֹ כִּגְבוֹהַּ שָׁמַיִם
מֵאָרֶץ⁵ᵃ, וְהוּא לְהַרְחִיק הָרוּחָנִיּוּת מֵהַגַּשְׁמִיּוּת, וּלְהַבְדִּיל
בֵּינֵיהֶם זֶהוּ עַל יְדֵי אוֹמְרוֹ: כְּהַבְדֵּל שֶׁבֵּין שָׁמַיִם שֶׁהוּא
הַנִּרְאֶה לְעַיִן גַּשְׁמִית מְרוֹמָם וְנִבְדָּל מִן הָאָרֶץ שֶׁהוּא דָּבָר
הַיּוֹתֵר שָׁפָל וְהַיּוֹתֵר תַּחַת, כֵּן כָּל דְּבָרִים הָרוּחָנִים כְּמוֹ
הַמַּלְאָכִים וּכְלָלִיּוּת בְּיַ״ע רוּחָנִיִּים זֶהוּ לַהֲוָיֵי' שֶׁהוּא הַמַּנְהִיגָם
בְּהַשְׁגָּחָה פְּרָטִיּוֹת,

אָמְנָם הָאָרֶץ וְכָל אֲשֶׁר בָּהּ, הִנֵּה מִצַּד הֱיוֹתָם עֲלוּלִים
הַיּוֹתֵר שְׁפֵלִים, הֲרֵי זֶה הַשְׁפָּלָה לְפָנָיו יִתְבָּרֵךְ לְהַשְׁפִּיל אֶת
עַצְמוֹ לְהַשְׁגִּיחַ בָּהֶם הַשְׁגָּחָה פְּרָטִית, וְלָכֵן נָתַן הַכֹּחַ
לְהַמַּזָּלוֹת וְשָׂרִים שֶׁלְּמַעְלָה, שֶׁיִּהְיוּ הֵם הַמַּנְהִיגִים
וְהַמַּשְׁגִּיחִים כְּפִי רְצוֹנָם וְאַוַּת נַפְשָׁם, אֲשֶׁר נָתַן הוּא יִתְבָּרֵךְ
בָּהֶם כֹּחַ כוּ' לְהַשְׁגִּיחַ הַשְׁגָּחָה פְּרָטִית בְּכָל פְּרָטֵי דְּבָרִים
הַנִּמְצָאִים בַּעֲלוּלִים הַשְּׁפֵלִים אֲשֶׁר בָּאָרֶץ הַגַּשְׁמִי שֶׁלְּמַטָּה,

וְזֶהוּ וְהָאָרֶץ נָתַן לִבְנֵי אָדָם כוּ', וְזֶהוּ עִנְיַן אֱלֹקָא

---

house. Four stages are necessary: 1) A general idea, as yet undefined; 2) A definite idea of the house in one's mind; 3) The architectural plan or design; 4) The actual building of the house (*Tanya*, Bilingual Edition, p. 343, fn. 3; p. 844 (Kehot, 1998)).

"Higher" (or "Supernal") and "Lower" refer to stages closer or more distant from the Creator, with a greater or lesser awareness of Him (not, of course, implying physical distance). Lower Worlds appear to be independent entities apart from the Creator.

(Through the performance of *mitzvot* and subordination of the physical world to the divine purpose, all Worlds are elevated, and experience a clearer apprehension of

G-d. See J. Immanuel Schochet, *Mystical Concepts in Chassidism*, Ch. 2 (*Tzimtzum*) and Ch. 4 (Worlds).)

35. HASHGACHA PRATIT, in the Hebrew. Often conceptually translated as Divine Providence, for it conveys the idea of G-d's attention and care for detail, in our context, however, the literal translation of "detailed supervision" is more fitting.

36. Deuteronomy 10:14.

37. In a transcriber's notes of the discourse: "As our Sages said (*Bereshit Rabbah* 10:6), 'There is no blade of grass below that does not have a *mazal* above that strikes it and says to it, Grow!'"

man and the concept of [G-d being] "G-d of gods." The "gods" referred to are the ministering angels and the constellations which, according to [the idolaters'] erroneous thinking, are the providers of spiritual influence to the world and its inhabitants; for this reason, [the idolaters] worship them.[38]

For example, [in] the land of Greece,[39] which receives its vitality through the constellation Virgo,[40] women often served as heads of state and were deified,[41] since, to the idolaters' thinking, these [women] were [the embodiment of those gods who were] providing the flow of vitality to their land.[42]

(Although it is true that every influx [of vitality] to a land does indeed pass through the leader who rules and governs that land,[43] nevertheless, [this influx] simply passes on *through* him. He himself is not the provider or source of the vitality. Rather, it can be compared to a craftsman who performs his labor with tools. Although [it seems as if] the tools carry out the actual work, it is in fact the craftsman who *employs* the tools; after all, it is the craftsman, and not his tools, who receive the praise for being the wondrous craftsman who produced such a wondrous masterpiece.

Along these same lines, we can understand the concept that, although [the flow of vitality] does indeed pass through the ministering angel, he is like a craftsman's tool. Although the craftsman's creative capacity must be channeled through the tool in order to be realized, the tool itself is due no credit at all.[44])

---

38. Rather than worshipping only G-d, the Source of the energy transmitted through the constellations and ministering angels.

39. *Yavan*, the Biblical name for Greece, is sometimes used to refer to the Hellenistic culture generally, rather than to Greece specifically. The Ptolemaic queens of Hellenistic Egypt often co-ruled with their husbands (who were also their brothers). Bere-

nice III and Berenice IV were the sole heads of state; Cleopatra V co-ruled with her daughter, Berenice IV, for a year before her death. Cleopatra VII co-ruled with several husbands but effectively ruled the empire alone.

40. See *Rabbenu Bachya* on Deuteronomy 31:16, "It has been said in the books of wisdom...the lands of Ishmael receive their vitality through the constellation Scorpio, Persia

דְּאֶלָקַיָּא, פֵּירוּשׁ אֱלָקַיָּא הֵם הַשָּׂרִים וְהַמַּזָּלוֹת, שֶׁלְדַעְתָּם
וְטָעוּתָם הִנֵּה הֵם הֵם הַמַּשְׁפִּיעִים לָאָרֶץ וְלַדָּרִים עָלֶיהָ וְלָכֵן
הֵם עוֹבְדִים אוֹתָם,

וּכְמוֹ שֶׁבְּאֶרֶץ יָוָן, שֶׁהַשְׁפָּעַת חִיּוּתָם הוּא מִמַּזַּל בְּתוּלָה,
וְלָכֵן עַל הָרוֹב נְקֵבוֹת הֵם הַמַּנְהִיגִים אֶת הַמְּלוּכָה, וְקוֹרִים
אוֹתָם אֱלָקוּת[כ], שֶׁלְפִי דַעְתָּם הֵם הֵם הַמַּשְׁפִּיעִים חַיּוּת
בָּאָרֶץ הַהִיא.

(וַהֲגַם כִּי בֶּאֱמֶת כָּל הַשְׁפָּעָה שֶׁנִּשְׁפָּע בָּאָרֶץ עוֹבֵר דֶּרֶךְ
הַמּוֹשֵׁל הַמּוֹשֵׁל[כד] וְשׁוֹלֵט[כג] עַל הָאָרֶץ הַהִיא, אַךְ הִנֵּה זֶהוּ
רַק מַה שֶׁעוֹבֵר עַל יָדוֹ, אֲבָל אֵינֶנּוּ הוּא עַצְמוֹ הַמַּשְׁפִּיעַ
וְהַגּוֹרֵם בָּזֶה, כִּי אִם עַל דֶּרֶךְ הָאוּמָן שֶׁפּוֹעֵל פְּעוּלָתוֹ עַל
יְדֵי הַכֵּלִים, הֲגַם כִּי הָעוֹשִׂים הֵם הַכֵּלִים, אָמְנָם הוּא עַל יְדֵי
הָאוּמָן הַפּוֹעֵל עַל יְדֵי הַכֵּלִים, וַהֲרֵי מְשַׁבְּחִים אֶת הָאוּמָן
שֶׁהוּא אוּמָן מוּפְלָא שֶׁעָשָׂה מְלָאכָה מוּפְלָאת כָּזֶה, וְלֹא הַכֵּלִים
הַפּוֹעֲלִים,

וְעַל דֶּרֶךְ זֶה יוּבַן, הֲגַם כִּי עוֹבֵר דֶּרֶךְ הַשַּׂר כו' עִם כָּל
זֶה הֲרֵי הוּא כִּכְלֵי הָאוּמָן שֶׁאוּמָן פּוֹעֵל עַל יָדוֹ, שֶׁדֶּרֶךְ
מַעֲבַר הַכְּלִי עוֹבֵר הַכֹּחַ הַנַּעֲשֶׂה וְנִפְעָל, וְעִם כָּל זֶה אֵינוֹ
מִתְיַיחֵס לְהַכְּלִי כְּלָל,)

through the constellation Sagittarius, the Philistines through Capricorn, and Edom through Virgo or Libra."

41. See also *Maamarei Admur Hazaken, Inyanim*, p. 383.

42. Because Virgo, the maiden, is a feminine symbol, female rulers were deified as human embodiments of the constellation.

43. See *Iggeret Hakodesh*, 25 (139b); *Shaarei Teshuvah*, 6a, fn. 3; *Maamarei Admur HaEmtza'ee, Devarim*, vol. 1, p. 164, where it is further referenced.

44. Regarding all of this, see also *Kuntres UMaayan*, Discourses Twenty-three & Twenty-four (in English (Kehot, 2006): *Overcoming Folly*, p. 324 ff., pp. 342-44).

In saying that the Creator is the "G-d of gods," [the idolaters] offer the interpretation that, while He is their [ultimate] source [of vitality], He does not rule over or govern the world at all. Instead, they claim that He is the G-d of gods, for *the earth He gave...*[45] meaning, the ministering angels and constellations are the ones that manage the earth, since for Him to do so would be degrading, as previously explained. G-d is so exalted, in the sense of being lofty and exalted, that *His glory transcends the heavens,*[46] as has likewise been explained above.

This is what Pharaoh meant when he said, *I know not the L-rd*: "He has no relation whatsoever to me, inasmuch as He is lofty, and so on, and has abandoned the management of the world to the constellations and ministering angels. Therefore, *Who is the L-rd that I should listen to Him?*" [Pharaoh reasoned that G-d would surely not intervene] to change the terrestrial status quo, i.e., his harsh enslavement of the Jews, and have them sent away from his presence to serve G-d in the wilderness. As such, *I will not release the Israelites.*

3.

A FUNDAMENTAL ERROR

This is truly an erroneous belief, for He *who dwells on High* is the very One who *looks down so low upon heaven and earth.*[47] Accordingly, the Jews, who are "believers, the children of believers"[48] that "there is no constellation for the Jews,"[49] know

---

45. In this reading, the second phrase of the verse describes G-d's relinquishing of terrestrial affairs to His appointees.

46. Cf. Psalms 113:4. See above, fn. 31.

47. Psalms 113:5-6. See also below, end of discourse; *Siddur im Dach, Shaar Tefillat Rosh Hashanah,* 237c; *Maamarei Admur HaEmtza'ee, Devarim,* vol. 3, p. 1035; *Torat Chaim,*

Vayechi 244d ff.

48. See *Shabbat* 97a. See also *Or Hatorah, Bereshit,* vol. 3, p. 1104; ibid., *Tisa* p. 1879. This is an expression referring to an innate spiritual characteristic possessed by every Jew. By virtue of a spiritual inheritance transmitted through the soul, the Jew intuitively senses that G-d attends to all of the affairs of man.

49. See *Shabbat* 156a. See also *Maa-*

וְאוֹמְרִים שֶׁהַבּוֹרֵא יִתְבָּרֵךְ הוּא אֱלָקָא דֶאֱלָקַיָּא, פֵּירוּשׁ
שֶׁהוּא הַמָּקוֹר לָהֶם, אֲבָל אֵינוֹ מוֹשֵׁל וְשׁוֹלֵט כְּלָל בָּאָרֶץ,
רַק אֱלָקָא דֶאֱלָקַיָּא בִּלְבַד, כִּי הָאָרֶץ נָתַן כו' שֶׁהַשָּׂרִים שֶׁל
מַעְלָה וְהַמַּזָּלוֹת הֵם יַנְהִגוּ אֶת הָאָרֶץ, מִפְּנֵי שֶׁהוּא הַשְּׁפָלָה
לְפָנָיו יִתְבָּרֵךְ כַּנַּ"ל, לָכֵן הוּא רָם בִּבְחִינַת רוֹמְמוּת
וְהִתְנַשְּׂאוּת, אֲשֶׁר עַל כֵּן עַל הַשָּׁמַיִם לָרוּם כְּבוֹדוֹכה כו' וְכַנַּ"ל.

וְזֶהוּ שֶׁאָמַר פַּרְעֹה לֹא יָדַעְתִּי אֶת הוי', שֶׁאֵינוֹ שַׁיָּיךְ לִי
כְּלָל לִהְיוֹתוֹ בִּבְחִינַת רָם כו' וְעָזַב הַהַנְהָגָה הַשַּׁיָּיכָה לָאָרֶץ
בִּידֵי הַמַּזָּלוֹת וְהַשָּׂרִים, וְאִם כֵּן מִי הוי' אֲשֶׁר אֶשְׁמַע בְּקוֹלוֹ,
לְשַׁנּוֹת הַהַנְהָגָה שֶׁלְּמַטָּה שֶׁיִּשְׂרָאֵל הָיוּ נְתוּנִים אֶצְלוֹ
בַּעֲבוֹדָה קָשָׁה, לְשַׁלְּחָם מֵעַל פָּנָיו שֶׁיַּעַבְדוּ אֶת ה' בַּמִּדְבָּר,
וְלָכֵן לֹא אֲשַׁלַּח אֶת יִשְׂרָאֵל כו'.

ג.

אָמְנָם בֶּאֱמֶת טָעוּת הוּא אֶצְלָם, וְהַמַּגְבִּיהִי לָשֶׁבֶת הִנֵּה
הוּא מַשְׁפִּילִיכו לִרְאוֹת בַּשָּׁמַיִם וּבָאָרֶץ בְּשָׁוֶה, וְלָכֵן יִשְׂרָאֵל
מַאֲמִינִים בְּנֵי מַאֲמִינִיםכז שֶׁאֵין מַזָּל לְיִשְׂרָאֵלכח יוֹדְעִים

---

marei Admur HaEmtza'ee, Shemot, vol. 2, p. 380, where it is referenced further.

Each nation possesses a guardian angel who serves as the conduit for the flow of vitality. There are Seventy Ministering Angels that actually correspond to the Seventy Nations of the ancient world from which all modern nations descend. The Jews, who are not included in this count—as in the expression, "one lamb surrounded by seventy wolves" (*Tanchuma, Toldot* 5; *Esther Rabbah* 10:11; *Pesikta Rabbatai*, Ch. 9)—do not have a specific guardian angel through which G-dly energy is channeled to them. Rather,

they receive their vitality and sustenance directly from G-d. See *Iggeret Haakodesh*, 25, from *Tikkunei Zohar*, 32 (76b).

(Chasidus interprets this statement homiletically, that instead of reading it *ein mazal l'Yisrael*, which means "there is no constellation for the Jews," it is read *ayin mazal l'Yisrael*, that the conduit from which the Jewish people receive vitality is the Divine state of *ayin*, lit., "nothingness," so termed for it surpasses the comprehension of created beings (*Or Torah* #147; *Likkutei Torah, Haazinu* 71d; *Shemini Atzeret* 83b).)

and believe in *hashgacha pratit*[34]—that G-d supervises in detail[50] all that transpires on the earth, as well as in the waters below the earth.[51]

This is what Moses meant, after [G-d] afflicted Pharaoh and all of Egypt, when he said: *You should know that there is none other like Me in the whole world*,[52] emphasizing "in the *whole* world." This is also what is meant by the verse, *in order that they should speak highly of My name in the whole world*.[53] This was in order to eradicate from them their erroneous belief that *G-d has abandoned the world* and relegated its sole management to the constellations, leaving Himself to play no role whatsoever [in its management].

Just the opposite is true: *There is none other like Me in the whole world*, and no one can challenge G-d's ability to alter the order of nature here on earth.[54] This is the [fundamental] belief and knowledge of the Jewish people, who believe in and know that which they received through our teacher Moses [directly] from the mouth of G-d, namely, to *Know this day and take unto your heart that* Havaya *is* Elokim; *in the heavens above and upon the earth below there is nothing else.*[55]

---

50. The Jewish position fundamentally rejects the role of actual intermediaries. While, to be sure, such channels do exist, they are not distinct entities independent of G-d and, as such, do not stand instead of or preclude His involvement in worldly affairs. He has not delegated them with authority, but rather, uses them as mere tools, as in the metaphor of the craftsman and his tools employed earlier, and also later in the discourse.

51. A term borrowed from Exodus 20:4. In discussing this point, *Maamarei Admur Hazaken, Inyanim*, p. 385, cites the following sources as further support-text: Exodus 8:18; cf. Daniel 4:32; Psalms 38:23; *Chullin*

7b; Jeremiah 32:19; cf. Zechariah 4:10; II Chronicles 16:9.

52. Exodus 9:14.

53. Ibid. 9:16.

54. In a transcriber's notes of the discourse: "The words *in the whole world* are seemingly superfluous, for the main point here is to know that there is none other like G-d. However, the Egyptians, too, agree that G-d is the Manager over the heavens, but they are in denial when they maintain that *He relinquished [responsibility for] the earth*. Therefore, G-d wrought miracles and wonders on earth, changing the earth's nature according to His wish and desire. In this manner the

3160 (5/11)

SICK CALL REQUEST FORM

Date: _____

Name: _____ DIN: _____

Cell Location: _____ Work Location: _____

☐ **If in keeplock status, check this box.** ☐ **Request interpreter at encounter**

☐ I request to be seen at sick call.

Reason For Sick Call Request: * _____ *Garlic*

2 Boxes Drinks _____ *Romaine*

Apple Onions - Bag _____ *Tomatoes*

1 lb Moz _____ *Cucumber*

1 lb cheddar _____ *Peppers (2)*

2 cans mushrooms _____

Chocolate _____

Hard Candy _____

☐ Medication Refill Only. Not Requesting Sick Call Visit.

Medication: *black Bread*   Prescription #: _____

_____   _____

_____   _____

_____   _____

_____   _____

☐ Other: _____

_____

_____

_____

* If reason is not provided, you will be seen at next scheduled sick call.

Estado de Nueva York
Departamento de Correcciones y Supervisión Comunitaria

FORMULARIO DE PETICIÓN PARA LA CITA POR ENFERMEDAD

Fecha: _____

Nombre: _____ DIN: _____

Ubicación Celda: _____ Ubicación Trabajo: _____

☐ **Escoja si está bajo Encierro.**   ☐ **Solicito intérprete durante cita.**

☐ Solicito que me atiendan en una Cita por Enfermedad.

Razón para solicitar la Cita: * _____

_____

_____

_____

_____

_____

_____

_____

_____

☐ Sólo Renovación de Medicamento. No solicito Cita por Enfermedad.

Medicamento: Receta No:

_____   _____

_____   _____

_____   _____

_____   _____

_____   _____

☐ Otro: _____

_____

_____

_____

_____

* Si no ofrece razón, lo atenderán en la próxima Cita por Enfermedad programada.

State of New York
Department of Corrections and Community Supervision

SICK CALL REQUEST FORM

Date: _____

Name: _____ DIN: _____

Cell Location: _____ Work Location: _____

☐ **If in keeplock status, check this box.**   ☐ **Request interpreter at encounter**

☐ I request to be seen at sick call.

Reason For Sick Call Request: * _____

_____

_____

_____

_____

_____

_____

_____

☐ Medication Refill Only. Not Requesting Sick Call Visit.

Medication: Prescription #:

_____   _____

_____   _____

_____   _____

_____   _____

_____   _____

☐ Other: _____

_____

_____

_____

_____

* If reason is not provided, you will be seen at next scheduled sick call.

Estado de Nueva York
Departamento de Correcciones y Supervisión Comunitaria

FORMULARIO DE PETICIÓN PARA LA CITA POR ENFERMEDAD

Fecha: _____

Nombre: _____ DIN: _____

Ubicación Celda: _____ Ubicación Trabajo: _____

☐ **Escoja si está bajo Encierro.** ☐ **Solicito intérprete durante cita.**

☐ Solicito que me atiendan en una Cita por Enfermedad.

Razón para solicitar la Cita: * _____

_____

_____

_____

_____

_____

_____

_____

☐ Sólo Renovación de Medicamento. No solicito Cita por Enfermedad.

Medicamento: Receta No:

_____   _____

_____   _____

_____   _____

_____   _____

_____   _____

☐ Otro: _____

_____

_____

_____

* Si no ofrece razón, lo atenderán en la próxima Cita por Enfermedad programada.

וּמַאֲמִינִים בְּהַשְׁגָּחָתוֹ יִתְבָּרֵךְ בִּבְחִינַת הַשְׁגָּחָה פְּרָטִיּוּת עַל כָּל דָּבָר שֶׁלְּמַטָּה בָאָרֶץ וַאֲשֶׁר בַּמַּיִם מִתַּחַת לָאָרֶץ,

וְזֶהוּ שֶׁאָמַר מֹשֶׁה בְּהַכּוֹתוֹ אֶת פַּרְעֹה וְכָל מִצְרַיִם, לְמַעַן תֵּדַע שֶׁאֵין כָּמוֹנִי בְּכָל הָאָרֶץﬨﬨ, בְּכָל הָאָרֶץ דַּוְקָא, וְכֵן לְמַעַן סַפֵּר שְׁמִי בְּכָל הָאָרֶץﬧ, שֶׁזֶּהוּ לְהוֹצִיא מִדַּעְתָּם וְטָעוּתָם שֶׁעָזַב ה' אֶת הָאָרֶץ שֶׁיִּתְנַהֲגוּ עַל יְדֵי הַמַּזָּלוֹת לְבָד וְאֵין לוֹ יִתְבָּרֵךְ חֵלֶק בָּזֶה,

כִּי אִם שֶׁאֵין כָּמוֹנִי בְּכָל הָאָרֶץ דַּוְקָא שֶׁיִּמְחֶה בְּיָדוֹ לְשַׁנּוֹת טֶבַע וְהַהַנְהָגָה אֲשֶׁר בָּאָרֶץ דַּוְקָא, וּכְמוֹ אֱמוּנַת וְדַעַת יִשְׂרָאֵל שֶׁהֵם מַאֲמִינִים וְיוֹדְעִים כְּמוֹ שֶׁמְּקוּבָּלִים מִמֹּשֶׁה רַבֵּנוּ עָלָיו הַשָּׁלוֹם מִפִּי הַגְּבוּרָה וְיָדַעְתָּ הַיּוֹםﬧﬧ וַהֲשֵׁבֹתָ אֶל לְבָבֶךָ כִּי הוי' הוּא הָאֱלֹקִים בַּשָּׁמַיִם מִמַּעַל וְעַל הָאָרֶץ מִתַּחַת אֵין עוֹד,

Egyptians would come to the realization that G-d is also the Manager of the earth. Hence the words, *in the whole world.*"

55. Deuteronomy 4:39.
HAVAYA/ELOKIM. *Havaya* and *Elokim* are two of the seven primary divine names mentioned in Scripture. (*Havaya* is the colloquial form—in Kabbalah and *Chakirah* (Torah philosophy)—of the Ineffable Divine Name, or Tetragrammaton, Y-H-V-H. The letters are rearranged so as not to pronounce the sacred Name.)

Each divine name expresses a different aspect or attribute of the Divinity (see *Shemot Rabbah* 3:6).

The name of *Keil*, for example, refers to G-d in His attribute of kindness, *Elokim* refers to G-d in His attribute of justice, while *Havaya* refers to G-d in His attribute of mercy (see *Rashi* to Genesis 1:1).

Chasidus explains the difference between *Havaya* and *Elokim* thus: *Havaya* refers to G-d the Infinite, transcending creation and nature, time and space completely—the level of Divinity that brings everything into existence *ex nihilo*. The name *Elokim* represents the level of G-dliness which conceals the infinite light and life-force, as this infinite force is too intense for finite creatures to endure. *Elokim* is the power of G-d that makes the world appear as though it exists naturally and independently by itself. *Elokim* therefore has the same numerical value as *hateva*, the Hebrew word for "nature."

Thus, in stating that *Havaya* is *Elokim*, the Torah makes clear that one and the same G-d is both transcen-

Indeed, this also explains Pharaoh's question, "Who is
Havaya?": [He specifically used the name *Havaya*, for] he was
already familiar with [G-dliness as manifested in the name]
Elokim.[56]

TWO MODES OF DIVINE INTERACTION: *HAVAYA* AND *ELOKIM*

The name *Elokim* connotes might and power,[57] as in *the
mighty ones of the land.*[58] Thus [when interpreting Pharaoh's
dream] Joseph said, Elokim *will provide for Pharaoh's welfare,*[59] for he understood that to [Pharaoh's] thinking, it was
axiomatic that the power[60] that provided him with vitality
should also be the one to provide for [his] welfare.[61]

But in truth, *Havaya* and *Elokim* are [of] the same [es-
sence].[62] The powers which provide [the flow of vitality] are
indistinguishable from *Havaya,*[63] for *it is He*[64] *who gives power
to succeed,*[65] and it is He who supervises in detail *over all the
ways of men, to repay each man according to his ways and the
outcome of his deeds*[66]—albeit through the ministering angels

---

dent of creation and immanently involved in even its most mundane and
natural phenomena.

And *there is nothing else* confirms
that all of the appointed conduits for
the flow of G-d's creative energy to
the world are truly naught, con-
stituting no independent existence for
themselves.

56. See *Torah Or, Miketz* 43a; *Siddur
im Dach, Shaar Hachanukah* 271b.
Pharaoh was aware only of G-d as expressed in the natural world. He thus
attributed divinity directly to G-d's
intermediaries that purvey the flow of
life force to it, while regarding the
aspect of G-d that transcends the natural world as remote and abstract, ex-
erting no power over earthly events.

57. See *Shulchan Aruch Harav, Orach
Chaim* 5:3; *Torat Chaim, Vaera* 75b,

where it is further referenced.

58. Ezekiel 17:13. The words *Elokim*
and *eilei* ("mighty") share the same
root—"*eil.*" In the context of this
verse, it is not used as a divine name,
but as a description of human strength.

59. Genesis 41:16.

60. That is, divine power as expressed
only by the name *Elokim.*

61. Pharaoh understood the dream to
be an indication for some course of
action to be taken in regards to the
administration of Egypt's practical affairs. Joseph thus deliberately used
the divine name which refers to G-d
as a supreme force within nature, for
if he had used the name which describes G-d as being a supernatural,
transcendent Being, Pharaoh would

פֵּירוּשׁ, כִּי פַּרְעֹה אָמַר מִי הוי' כו', אֲבָל מִשֵּׁם אֱלֹקִים
יָדַע[62],

וְהַיְינוּ כִּי עֶצֶם פֵּירוּשׁ לְשׁוֹן שֵׁם אֱלֹקִים הוּא לְשׁוֹן כֹּחַ[63]
וִיכוֹלֶת כְּמוֹ וְאֶת אֵילֵי הָאָרֶץ[64], וּכְמוֹ שֶׁאָמַר לוֹ יוֹסֵף
אֱלֹקִים יַעֲנֶה אֶת שְׁלוֹם פַּרְעֹה[65], שֶׁהֵבִין לְפִי דַעְתּוֹ שֶׁהַכֹּחַ
הַמַּשְׁפִּיעַ לוֹ יַעֲנֶה שְׁלוֹמוֹ כו',

אָמְנָם בֶּאֱמֶת הוי' הוּא הָאֱלֹקִים, שֶׁכָּל כֹּחוֹת אֵלוּ
הַמַּשְׁפִּיעִים הֵם הֵם עַצְמָם הוי' שֶׁהוּא הַנּוֹתֵן לְךָ כֹּחַ לַעֲשׂוֹת
חָיִל[66], וְהוּא הוּא הַמַּשְׁגִּיחַ בְּהַשְׁגָּחָה פְּרָטִית עַל כָּל דַּרְכֵי בְּנֵי
אָדָם, לָתֵת לְאִישׁ כִּדְרָכָיו וְכִפְרִי מַעֲלָלָיו[66] עַל יְדֵי הַשָּׂרִים

---

have taken no comfort, believing this aspect of G-d far too lofty to have any bearing on worldly matters. See also above, fn. 55.

In a transcriber's notes of the discourse: "Pharaoh was aware of the name *Elokim*, for Joseph had informed him of *Elokim*, as the verse states. Joseph had informed Pharaoh of *Elokim* in its unified state with *Havaya*, but Pharaoh mistakenly accepted only the name *Elokim*, and denied the name *Havaya*. Therefore, G-d performed the miracles and wonders in his land, changing the laws of nature unopposed."

62. See *Zohar*, Intro, 12a; II:161a ff. *Maamarei Admur HaEmtza'ee, Devarim*, vol. 1, p. 175, and sources cited there; *Torat Chaim, Vaera* 60a; *Torat Shmuel—Sefer 5633*, vol. 2, p. 405 ff.

63. Although there is an intermediating system in place through which *Havaya* affects the phen-omenological world, this system is not separate from Him, but part of his Oneness.

See *Tanya*, end Ch. 21: "The process [represented by the name *Elokim*] by which *Havaya* conceals itself is not an entity apart from [*Havaya*], forefend, but rather like the snail whose shell comes from its very own body, as it is stated, *Havaya is Elokim* ...and therefore all is literally as naught before Him." See also *Shaar Hayichud v'haEmunah*, end Ch. 7: "Before the Holy One, all is literally as naught before Him, like a ray from the sun while still within the sun, for His attribute of self-screening [as embodied by the name *Elokim*] does not pose an interposition for Him, forefend, because it is not an entity unto itself, rather *Havaya is Elokim*."

64. *Havaya*—the Name used in this verse.

65. Deuteronomy 8:18.

66. Jeremiah 32:19.

and powers, which transmit vitality like an axe in the hands of the woodchopper."[67]

This is the meaning of the verse, *in the heavens above and upon the earth below there is nothing else*: Just as *in the heavens above*—which even the idolaters concede—is the abode of His glory and is privy to His detailed supervision, so, too, *upon the earth below there is nothing else* at all. Namely, the power of a ministering angel or other purveyor of vitality— even the likes of the angel Matat,[68] called "Minister of the Universe"[69]—is not something "else" besides G-d's essence. There is nothing else at all, for there is literally nothing besides Him.

THE AXE IN THE HANDS OF THE WOODCHOPPER

[The role of the ministering angels] may be compared to that of an axe, which has no significance of its own without the woodchopper who uses it. The axe has no choice over what it does or does not do. The generalities and specifics of how the axe is used are entirely up to the woodchopper's artistic vision and manual dexterity.

The work is not at all attributable to the tool, but rather to the craftsman who acts through the tool.

—As for the saying, "A craftsman without tools is no [craftsman],"[70] the meaning is not that the actual work of the craftsman is attributed to the tool, but that without the tool, the ability and proficiency of the craftsman cannot be actualized, and thus it would effectively be *as if* he were not [a craftsman].—

We may understand [the significance of] all the specific categories of physical creation—inanimate, vegetative, animal and human—in a similar manner.[71]

---

67. *Moreh Nevuchim* III, Ch. 29; *Zohar* I:31:1; Isaiah 10:15. See also above, fn. 42.

68. MATAT. Matat's full name is Matatron, but it is customary that his name not be pronounced in full, for, as the *Zohar* (III:282b) states, he is G-d's servant, the first creature created by G-d, and the ruler of all His heavenly legions. In addition, *Rashi* on Exodus 23:21 writes that "his name is similar to the name of his Creator"—the numerical value of Matatron being equivalent to the Divine Name שׁ-ד-י. Nevertheless, he, too, is no more than a

וְהַכֹּחוֹת הַמַּשְׁפִּיעִים, שֶׁהֵם כַּגַּרְזֶן בְּיַד הַחוֹצֵב[לה] בּוֹ כו',

וְזֶהוּ שֶׁאָמַר בַּשָּׁמַיִם מִמַּעַל וּבָאָרֶץ מִתַּחַת אֵין עוֹד, פֵּירוּשׁ שֶׁכְּמוֹ בַּשָּׁמַיִם מִמַּעַל, גַּם לְפִי דִבְרֵיכֶם, שָׁם מִשְׁכַּן כְּבוֹדוֹ וְהַשְׁגָּחָתוֹ הַפְּרָטִיוֹת, כֵּן גַּם בָּאָרֶץ מִתַּחַת אֵין עוֹד כְּלָל כו', פֵּירוּשׁ אֵין עוֹד, שֶׁבְּחִינַת הַכֹּחַ שֶׁל הַמַּזָּל וְהַשַּׂר הַמַּשְׁפִּיעַ כְּמוֹ מְטַטְ"ט שֶׁהוּא שָׂרוֹ שֶׁל עוֹלָם[לט] אֵינוֹ נֶחְשָׁב כְּלָל אֲפִילוּ לִבְחִינַת עוֹד שֶׁהוּא דָבָר נוֹסָף עַל עַצְמוּתוֹ, כִּי אִם אֵין עוֹד כְּלָל שֶׁאֵין דָּבָר נוֹסָף כְּלָל.

וְהַיְינוּ כְּמוֹ שֶׁהַגַּרְזֶן אֵינוֹ דָבָר נוֹסָף עַל הָאוּמָן הַפּוֹעֵל עַל יָדוֹ, וְהוּא מִפְּנֵי שֶׁאֵין לְהַגַּרְזֶן שׁוּם בְּחִירָה לַעֲשׂוֹת אוֹ שֶׁלֹּא לַעֲשׂוֹת, וְכָל הַבְּחִירָה בִּכְלָלִיּוּת עֲשִׂיָּיתוֹ אוֹ בִּפְרָטִיּוּת בְּטִיב עֲשִׂיּוֹתָיו הַכֹּל תָּלוּי בִּידֵי הָאוּמָן בְּאוֹפֶן הַשְׁגָּחָתוֹ וְטִיב אִימֵן יָדָיו כו',

וְלָכֵן אֵינוֹ מִתְיַיחֵס כְּלָל עֲשִׂיַּית הַדָּבָר לַכְּלִי הָעוֹשֵׂהוּ, כִּי אִם לַפּוֹעֵל הַפּוֹעֵל עַל יְדֵי הַכְּלִי,

– וּמַה שֶׁכָּתוּב אֵין אוּמָן בְּלֹא כֵלִים[ע], אֵין הַכַּוָּונָה לְיַחֵס עֶצֶם עֲשִׂיַּית הָאוּמָן לְהַכְּלִי, אֶלָּא שֶׁבְּלֹא הַכְּלִי אֵינוֹ יוֹצֵא מֵהֶעְלֵם אֶל הַגִּילּוּי בְּחִינַת כֹּחַ וְאִימֵן יַד הָאוּמָן, וַהֲרֵי הוּא כְּאִילוּ אֵינוֹ כו' –

וְעַל דֶּרֶךְ זֶה יוּבַן בְּכָל פְּרָטֵי דְבָרִים הַגַּשְׁמִיּוֹת בְּדוֹמֵם צוֹמֵחַ חַי מְדַבֵּר,

tool employed by G-d. (See *Sanhedrin* 38b for this reference and an interesting discussion between Rav Idit and a heretic regarding the very question of Matat being effectively divine.)

69. See *Yevamot* 16b, and *Tosfot* there.

70. See *Gevul Binyamin*, vol. 1, beg.,

where this is quoted from "the makers of parables." See also *Pri Megadim, Orach Chaim* (Intro.) in the first letter. This phrase implies that the tools are significant in their own right.

71. Just as the heavenly beings are not entities distinct from G-d, neither do the terrestrial creations constitute something additional to G-d.

Although each general category and each specific creation has its own degree of power and vitality, these do not constitute anything additional to G-d's Essence.[72] Rather, these powers are all themselves [expressions of] *Havaya*. For this reason, in the statement "*Havaya* is *Elokim*," the name *Elokim* is in the plural form,[73] signifying that the powers [that enliven] all species created, formed and made during the Six Days of Creation—as well as each specific creation, whether inanimate, vegetative, animal or human—are all [expressions of] *Havaya*. Even now, it is He who brings them into being exactly as when they were first created.[74]

Indeed, the verse *You give life to* (mechayeh) *them all*,[75] may alternatively be read[76] as "You give existence to (*mehaveh*) them all"[77] at every moment and every instant, as it says, "who in His goodness renews each day, continuously, the work of creation."[78] As explained elsewhere, [this renewal of creation is an expression] of his essential goodness, for "it is the nature of the benevolent to do good."[79] He renews [and re-enlivens] old things each day, continuously—and not just each day, but each moment; the daily renewal being slightly more recognizable,[80] as explained elsewhere.

---

72. In a transcriber's notes of the discourse: "They are thus not even called partners."

73. *Rashi* on Genesis 20:13, 35:7. See *Torah Or, Vaera* 56b; *Torat Chaim, Vaera* 60a ff; *Likkutei Torah, Emor* 31c. The plural form indicates that G-d provides a quality and quantity of energy that varies to befit each individual type of being.

74. See *Shaar Hayichud v'haEmunah*, Chs. 2 & 3; The Tzemach Tzedek's *Sefer Hachakirah*, 25b.

75. Nehemiah 9:6.

76. "So is cited in *Shaar Hayichud*

v'haEmunah, Ch. 2, and elsewhere in Chasidus. As of now, I have located it in *Pardes* 6:8...and in *Reshit Chochmah, Shaar Hakedushah*, Ch. 7, end; so it also appears in *Shaloh, Shaar HaOtiyot*, Discourse 3-4 (48b) and ibid., *Letter Samach* (70a)" (Footnote by the Lubavitcher Rebbe, *Sefer Hamaamarim 5704*, p. 20). In *Marei Mekomot, Hagahot, V'Heorot Ketzorot L'Shaar Hayichud v'haEmunah*, Ch. 2, the Rebbe notes: "Possibly these words are the Alter Rebbe's," and makes reference to the aforementioned *Pardes* and *Reshit Chochmah*.

77. The *Shaloh* and *Reshit Chochmah*, cited in the previous footnote, explain

עִם הֱיוֹת שֶׁיֵּשׁ לְכָל מִין בִּכְלָל, וּלְכָל אֶחָד וְאֶחָד בִּפְרַט
הַמִּין הַהוּא בִּפְרַט, כֹּחַ וְחַיּוּת פְּרָטִי, עִם כָּל זֶה אֵינֶנּוּ דָבָר
נוֹסָף עַל עַצְמוּתוֹ יִתְבָּרֵךְ, כִּי אִם הַכֹּחַ הַזֶּה עַצְמוֹ הוּא הוי׳,
שֶׁזֶּהוּ כַּוָּנַת אוֹמְרוֹ כִּי הוי׳ הוּא הָאֱלֹקִים לְשׁוֹן רַבִּיםמא,
שֶׁכָּל כֹּחוֹת הָרַבִּים בְּכָל מִינִים הַפְּרָטִים שֶׁנִּבְרְאוּ וְנוֹצְרוּ
וְנַעֲשׂוּ בְּשֵׁשֶׁת יְמֵי בְרֵאשִׁית, וְכֵן בְּכָל מִין פְּרָטֵי רַבּוֹת
נִבְרָאִים בְּדוֹמֵם צוֹמֵחַ חַי מְדַבֵּר, הַכֹּל הוּא הוי׳
הַמְהַוֶּוה אוֹתָם בִּתְחִילַּת בְּרִיאָתָם, וּכְמֵאָז כֵּן עַתָּה בִּלְתִּי שׁוּם
שִׁינּוּי כְּלָל,

וְאַל תִּקְרֵי מְחַיֶּה אֶלָּא מְהַוֶּוהמב בְּכָל עֵת וּבְכָל רֶגַע, וּכְמוֹ
שֶׁכָּתוּב וּבְטוּבוֹ מְחַדֵּשׁ בְּכָל יוֹם תָּמִיד מַעֲשֵׂה בְרֵאשִׁית,
וּכְמוֹ שֶׁכָּתוּב מִזֶּה בְּמָקוֹם אַחֵר שֶׁבְּטוּבוֹ הָעַצְמִי שֶׁבְּטֶבַע
הַטּוֹב לְהֵטִיבמד הוּא מְחַדֵּשׁ הַיְשָׁנִ[י]נוֹת בְּכָל יוֹם תָּמִיד כו׳,
וְלָאו דַּוְקָא בְּכָל יוֹם, אֶלָּא בְּכָל עֵת, רַק מִפְּנֵי שֶׁבְּכָל יוֹם
נִיכָּר קְצָת כְּמוֹ הִתְחַדְּשׁוּתמג כו׳ כְּמוֹ שֶׁכָּתוּב בְּמָקוֹם אַחֵר,

---

that although the verse uses the phrase *give life*, this does not mean that G-d only provides created beings with life in the way that the soul animates the already-existent body. Rather, the verse implies that this provision of life also serves to create them and to be responsible for their continued existence (*Lessons in Tanya, Shaar Hayichud v'haEmunah,* ad loc.).

The salient point is that since all creations are utterly dependent upon G-d for their very existence, they are truly non-entities and do not represent anything additional to G-d by virtue of their existence.

78. Liturgy, Blessings of the Shema (*Siddur Tehillat Hashem, Annotated Edition,* p. 41). See also comment by the author of the present discourse in *Or Hatorah, Bereshit,* vol. 6, p. 2040; *Torat Shmuel—Sefer 5636,* vol. 2, p. 251; *Sefer Hamaamarim 5678,* p. 120; *Torat Shmuel—Sefer 5640,* p. 416, where it is further referenced.

79. *Chacham Tzvi* (Responsa), sec. 18: *Shomer Emunim* 2:14, quoting Kabbalistic sources. *Emek Hamelech, Shaar Shaashuei Hamelech,* Ch. 1; *Shaar Hayichud v'haEmunah,* Ch. 4.

80. In a transcriber's notes of the discourse: "Although G-d renews the existence of creation each and every moment, the verse mentions the daily renewal of life force since it is more readily comprehensible to the human mind: At the beginning of creation, it

After stating "*Havaya* is *Elokim*," [the verse] intensifies the point[81] by explaining that *there is nothing else* besides His Essence; that is, no forces operate in partnership with G-d, as explained elsewhere.[82]

In order to negate that notion, the verse reiterates that *there is nothing else.*

Indeed, all the signs and wonders were brought upon Pharaoh and Egypt for this same purpose—to prove that *there is none like Me in the entire world*,[83] and by logical extension, *there is nothing else.*[84] These [signs and wonders] showed them that the ruling constellation of Egypt had no power to thwart or stand in opposition to G-d[85] and was by its very essence nothing additional [to G-d's existence], but rather like the plowshare used to plow, the axe used to chop and other similar analogies.

When [the Egyptians] beheld and recognized the greatness of G-d's miracles and the punishments to which they and their gods were sentenced,[86] they all believed [in the one Single G-d], albeit for the moment, for they saw that the ruling constellation of Egypt was powerless to oppose G-d and save them from His hand.[87] It is *the finger of G-d*[88] who is ruler and

---

was first dark and then it became light. When people see that this takes place every day, too, that first it's dark and then morning arrives, it becomes a given that G-d renews creation every day. In truth, however, the renewal of life force takes place each and every moment."

81. The verse first states that both the transcendent and immanent aspects of G-d are one. It then goes further and states that not only are both aspects of G-d one with each other, but that everything in existence is one with Him and that there are no other powers or forces outside of Him.

82. See *Mi Chamocha 5629* (in Eng-

lish: *True Existence* (Kehot, 2003), pp. 22-26), and sources cited there; *Sefer Hamaamarim Melukat*, vol. 1, p. 55.

In a transcriber's notes of the discourse: "The concept of partnership is as our Sages said (*Niddah* 31a), 'There are three partners in creating a human—the father, the mother, and G-d.' Although the father and mother's contributions are incomparable to that of G-d, they are nevertheless partners, for they chose to marry and procreate, when they had the ability to choose the opposite. By contrast, the heavenly hosts do not possess the ability to choose freely, and are merely as an axe in the hands of the woodchopper. The axe does not choose

וּלְהוֹסִיף וּלְחַזֵּק הַדָּבָר שֶׁאָמַר תְּחִלָּה, בֵּיאֵר כָּךְ אַחַר כָּךְ אֵין עוֹד, שֶׁאֵין שׁוּם עוֹד, הַיְינוּ דָּבָר נוֹסָף עַל עַצְמוּתוֹ כְּמוֹ עִנְיַן הַשִּׁיתּוּף[מה] שֶׁנִּתְבָּאֵר בְּמָקוֹם אַחֵר,

שֶׁבִּכְדֵי לְשַׁלֵּל גַּם דָּבָר זֶה אָמַר אֵין עוֹד כו',

וְעַל זֶה הָיוּ כָּל הָאוֹתוֹת וְהַמּוֹפְתִים שֶׁעָשׂוּ לְפַרְעֹה וּלְכָל מִצְרַיִם, לַאֲמֵת אֶצְלָם שֶׁאֵין כָּמוֹנִי בְּכָל הָאָרֶץ, וּמִמֵּילָא אֵין עוֹד, שֶׁהֲרֵי הֶרְאָה לָהֶם שֶׁאֵין כֹּחַ כְּלָל לִבְחִינַת מַזַּל מִצְרַיִם לִמְנוֹעַ וְלַעֲמוֹד נֶגְדוֹ יִתְבָּרֵךְ חָלִילָה, וְהוּא מִפְּנֵי כִּי בְּעֶצֶם אֵינוֹ דָּבָר נוֹסָף כְּלָל, כִּי אִם כְּמוֹ כְּלִי הַמַּחֲרֵישָׁה לַחֲרוֹשׁ בָּהֶם, וּכְלִי הַגַּרְזֶן לַחְצוֹב בּוֹ וְכַדוֹמֶה כו',

וּבְרִאוֹתָם כּוּלָם וְנִתְאַמֵּת אֶצְלָם עַל יְדֵי גוֹדֶל הַמַּפָּלוֹת שֶׁעָשָׂה ה' שְׁפָטִים בָּהֶם וּבֵאלֹקֵיהֶם, הֶאֱמִינוּ כּוּלָם לְפִי שָׁעָה עַל יְדֵי שֶׁרָאוּ שֶׁמַּזַּל מִצְרַיִם לֹא הָיָה יָכוֹל לְהִתְקוֹמֵם נֶגְדּוֹ

---

when to chop or when not to chop the wood...and therefore cannot be considered a 'partner.' ...Such is the status of the heavenly hosts."

83. Exodus 9:14.

84. The idolaters accept that G-d has sole authority in heaven. However, in the earthly realm, they believe that there are other powers that rule. Proving G-d's ultimate control over earthly happenings is thus a direct and wholesale refutation that any other power or authority exists.

85. In a transcriber's notes of the discourse: "For had the constellations any power to do as they wished, they would have opposed."

86. Cf. Exodus 12:12, Numbers 33:4.

87. In *Maamarei Admur Hazaken, Inyanim*, p. 385: "The constellation and ministering angels of Egypt are non-existent before Him, for everything is naught before Him." In *Or Hatorah, Tissa*, p. 1986: "It is only *His kingship* that *has dominion over all* (cf. Psalms 103:19), and this also explains the verse (Nehemiah 9:10), *You have made a name for Yourself to this day*: It became clear to all that He is G-d in the midst of the earth specifically, and *there is none else aside from Him* (Deuteronomy 4:35). The stars and constellations are merely as 'an ax in the hand of a woodchopper,' and He arranges them according to His will."

88. Exodus 8:15.

controller of all, even on this earth, and not, as they had erroneously believed, that He *has abandoned* [it, leaving its control for other forces].[89]

4.

Yet, the mixed multitude[15] sought to deny [G-d's dominion over the entire world] when Moshe "delayed" in his return from the mountain. They rebelled further by desiring that the Israelites also stray [from the true belief]. They exposited to the Jews [their explanation] that matters were just as they had seemed before [the Exodus]; that is, that the [true] managers of the world were indeed the constellations and ministering angels above.

Although Egypt had been stricken with plagues from which their ruling constellation could not help them, [the mixed multitude explained that] the punishment suffered by the [Egyptian] gods[85] was actually a proof in their favor, and occurred not as a result of G-d's management and detailed supervision, and not because *there is none else aside from Him*,[90] but rather for another reason.

There are twelve constellations in the sky,[91] and the ruling

---

89. In *Or Hatorah, Tissa,* pp. 1985-6: "In the cause and effect (*ilah* and *alul*) scenario, when the cause produces the effect, the cause is transformed from its prior state of being into its new role as an effect.

"The Egyptians erred in assuming that the creation of the world by G-d was in the manner of cause and effect. However, since in such a case, the cause is changed by being transformed into an effect, the Egyptians reasoned, "How is it possible for the Creator to be invested to the extent of dealing with physical creations? That would be a great transformation and degradation for G-d! Clearly, His glo-ry transcends the heavens, for they are spiritual effects, and will not influence Him as much, but He *has abandoned the earth* to the stars and constellations.

"In truth, however, the idea of cause and effect applies only in a lower realm. That is, in the evolvement of an animal's soul from the animalistic face of the divine Chariot (see Ezekiel 1:10). Similarly, "There is no blade of grass below that does not have a *mazal* above that strikes it and says to it, 'Grow!'" (*Bereshit Rabbah* 10:6). But the actual creation of the worlds was not in a manner of cause and effect, G-d forbid. G-d is called 'the Holy

יִתְבָּרֵךְ לְהַצִּילָם מִיָּדָם, אֵין זֶה כִּי אִם שֶׁאֲצַבַּע אֱלֹקִים הוּא הַמּוֹשֵׁל וְשׁוֹלֵט בַּכֹּל, הַיְינוּ גַּם בָּאָרֶץ כו׳, וְלֹא כְּפִי טָעוּתָם שֶׁעָזַב כו׳ כַּנַ״ל.

ד.

וְאָמְנָם הִנֵּה הָעֶרֶב רַב רָצוּ אַחַר כָּךְ לִכְפּוֹר בָּזֶה, כַּאֲשֶׁר בְּשֵׁשׁ מֹשֶׁה לָרֶדֶת מִן הָהָר, וְהוֹסִיפוּ סָרָה שֶׁרָצוּ שֶׁגַּם יִשְׂרָאֵל יָסוּרוּ, הִשְׁמִיעַ[מ] לְיִשְׂרָאֵל שֶׁהָאֱמֶת הוּא כַּאֲשֶׁר דִּימוּ מִתְּחִלָּה, שֶׁמַּנְהִיגֵי הָעוֹלָם הֵם הַמַּזָּלוֹת וְהַשָּׂרִים שֶׁלְּמַעְלָה כַּנַ״ל,

וּמַה שֶּׁלָּקוּ הַמִּצְרִים וְשֶׁלֹּא הָיָה בִּיכוֹלֶת הַמַּזָּל שֶׁלָּהֶם לְעוֹזְרָם, וְאַדְּרַבָּה שֶׁגַּם בֵּאלֹקֵיהֶם עָשָׂה שְׁפָטִים[מ], אֵין זֶה מֵחֲמַת שֶׁהַוִי׳ הוּא הַמַּנְהִיג בְּהַשְׁגָּחָה פְּרָטִיּוּת וְאֵין עוֹד מִלְּבַדּוֹ, כִּי אִם מִסִּיבָּה אַחֶרֶת,

וְהוּא כִּי יַעַן שֶׁיֵּשׁ י״ב מַזָּלוֹת בָּרָקִיעַ[מ], וּמַזַּל מִצְרַיִם הוּא

One, blessed be He,' for he is, in fact, holy and removed from all the worlds. Only a ray of G-d is upon the worlds—as in the verse (Psalms 145:13), *Your kingship is a kingship over all the worlds*— which is similar to the strength of a ray of sunlight in comparison to the sun. Just as the ray does not affect the sun in any way, so does the ray of G-d's light through which creation *ex nihilo* come about not affect G-d. In the daily morning service we say, "You are the same before the creation and You are the same since creation." Also, *I, G-d, have not changed* (Malachi 3:6). So it is not as in the manner of cause and effect, G-d forbid, where the cause becomes transformed into the effect.

"Moreover, the effect is compar-able to its cause. But this is not the case with G-d, for all His creations, whether spiritual or physical, are absolutely incomparable to Him at all. It is only once the worlds were created that the worlds interact with each other and there is an order of progression from the higher to the lower. This is all in the manner of 'an ax in the hand of a woodchopper,' and does not affect Him at all. And therefore, precisely because G-d dwells on high does He look down so low upon heaven and earth equally." This last point is discussed below, Ch. 5.

90. Deuteronomy 4:35.

91. See *Berachot* 32b; *Rambam, Hilchot Yesodei Hatorah* 3:6.

constellation of Egypt is Aries,[92] as Moses told Pharaoh, *Could we sacrifice the sacred animal of the Egyptians before their very eyes?*[93]

Now, the [real] purpose of the Passover offering was[94] that the Jews should slaughter the sheep[95]—[with all of its various legal stipulations, such as] *Do not break any of its bones*[96] and *Do not eat it [raw or cooked in water,] but only [roasted over a fire] including its head over its legs and internal organs*[97]—to completely invalidate [the distinct vitality of] the god of Egypt, the constellation of Aries. For this same reason, in the story of Joseph and his brothers, [the Torah] states *because the Egyptians were unable to eat with the Hebrews*[98] [as the Hebrews dined on sheep].

But the mixed multitude used cunning, declaring to the Jews that the constellation Taurus, the bull,[99] had battled the constellation of Aries, the sheep, and prevailed over it. We find this idea in the Book of Daniel[100]—and this is the sort of thing, [they argued,] that had taken place in Egypt, [proving] that the constellations are the ones who manage the earth. Therefore, [the mixed multitude] advised [the Jews] to make a molten calf, with the idea of entangling them in the worship of Taurus as, to their thinking, it had prevailed over Aries.[101]

---

92. The ram, an adult male sheep. See *Zohar* III:250b; ibid., I:256a.

93. Exodus 8:22. A reference to the paschal lamb.

94. See *Zohar* and *Ra'aya Mehemna* III:251a ff.

95. Cf. Exodus 12:6.

96. Ibid., verse 46.

97. Ibid., verse 9.

98. Genesis 43:32. See also *Targum Onkelus* there; *Likkutei Sichot*, vol. 5, p. 266, in footnote.

99. In *Or Hatorah, Tissa*, p. 1986: "which follows Aries."

100. Chs. 10-12. Daniel had a vision of the ministering angel of Babylonia, who described his war in heaven with the ministering angel of Persia.

101. In *Or Hatorah, Tissa*, p. 1986: "They therefore declared [see fn. 16],

מַזַּל טָלֶה‎מט‎, וּכְמוֹ שֶׁאָמַר מֹשֶׁה לְפַרְעֹה הֵן נִזְבַּח אֶת תּוֹעֲבַת מִצְרַיִם לְעֵינֵיהֶם‎נ‎ כו',

וְכַיָּדוּעַ שֶׁכָּל עִיקַר עִנְיַן מִצְוַת קָרְבַּן פֶּסַח‎נא‎ הָיָה בִּשְׁבִיל זֶה לִשְׁחוֹט שֶׁהֵּי‎נב‎, וְעֶצֶם לֹא תִשְׁבְּרוּ בוֹ‎נג‎, וְלֹא תֹאכְלוּ‎נד‎ כו' כִּי אִם רֹאשׁוֹ עַל כְּרָעָיו וְעַל קִרְבּוֹ, לְהַרְאוֹת אֵיךְ שֶׁאֵין מַמָּשׁ בֵּאלֹקֵי מִצְרַיִם שֶׁהוּא מַזַּל טָלֶה, וַאֲשֶׁר מִטַּעַם זֶה בְּסִיפּוּר מַעֲשֵׂה דְּיוֹסֵף עִם הַשְּׁבָטִים אָמַר גַּם כֵּן כִּי לֹא יוּכְלוּן הַמִּצְרִים לֶאֱכֹל עִם הָעִבְרִים‎נה‎,

וְהִתְחַכְּמוּ הָעֵרֶב רַב לְהַשְׁמִיעַ לְיִשְׂרָאֵל כִּי מַזַּל שׁוֹר הָיָה נִלְחָם בְּמִצְרַיִם עִם מַזַּל טָלֶה וְגָבַר עָלָיו, וְעַל דֶּרֶךְ שֶׁמָּצִינוּ שֶׁהַמַּזָּלוֹת נִלְחָמִים זֶה עִם זֶה כְּמוֹ שֶׁכָּתוּב בְּדָנִיֵּאל‎נו‎ כו', וְעַל דֶּרֶךְ זֶה הָיָה בְּמִצְרַיִם, אֲבָל מִכָּל מָקוֹם הַמַּנְהִיגִים בָּאָרֶץ הֵם הַמַּזָּלוֹת, וְלָכֵן יָעֲצוּ לָהֶם לַעֲשׂוֹת עֵגֶל מַסֵּכָה, וְהַכַּוָּונָה הוּא לְהַכְשִׁילָם שֶׁיַּעַבְדוּ לְמַזַּל שׁוֹר מִפְּנֵי כִּי לְפִי דַעְתָּם הוּא גָּבַר עַל מַזַּל טָלֶה.

Here is your god, O Israel, who took you out of Egypt, claiming that wasn't the hand of G-d that did it, but the power of the constellation Taurus, who was victorious over Aries, the constellation of Egypt.

"Thus, in Psalms 106[:20], the prophet complains, *They exchanged their Glory for the likeness of a grass-eating ox....* The constellations are ultimately rooted in the beasts of the divine Chariot (see Ezekiel 1:10). From there and down is where the concept of *ilah* and *alul* (cause and effect) comes into play (see above, fn. 88). Similarly, the root of Taurus is in the face of the ox of the Chariot. However, *They exchanged their Glory,* for in fact, it was G-d alone who had wrought all the awesome deeds and wonders, and it was the mixed multitude who attributed it to the power of Taurus, which is rooted in the face of the divine ox."

In a transcriber's notes of the discourse: "In truth, [the constellations] are unable to wage war themselves. The description of the constellations' battle in Daniel was due to the command of G-d, but on their own, they are powerless."

5.

SOULS FROM THE FEMININE PLANE

The women, however, rejected this [explanation] and did not participate with [the mixed multitude], refusing to give up their jewelry to make the calf.

This was because the source of their souls is in *nukva*,[102] and *His kingship has dominion over all*,[103] namely, *malchut* rules over all the seventy ministering angels in heaven.[104] [The women] knew and sensed in their souls that there was no substance to the constellations and ministering angels to a greater degree than did the men sense it, for the men's souls are from the masculine plane, *z'eyr anpin*[105] of *Atzilut*,[106] which is utterly

---

102. NUKVA. Literally, "female," this is another term for *malchut*, ("royalty" or "kingship") the tenth and last of the *sefirot*.

Kabbalistic literature abounds with allegorical human terms, and refers to categories represented by symbolic terms, such as "masculine" (generally: the emanating influencing aspect), and feminine (generally: the recipient aspect). See *Zohar* I:157b; cf. *Bava Batra* 74b; *Shomer Emunim* I:26f. These terms apply generally to the *sefirot*: *chochmah* is *abba* (father), *binah* is *imma* (mother), and the lower *sefirot* are the "children": from *chesed* to *yesod* as a whole correspond to *ben* (son); and *malchut* to bat (daughter). See *Zohar* III:290a ff; *Pardes Rimonim* 8:17. See further *Tanya*, Bilingual Edition, *Iggeret Hakodesh*, Sect. 20, note 62.

In the *Tikkunei Zohar* (intro. 17a), *malchut* is referred to as the "Mouth of G-d," the Word or Speech of G-d by which the world comes into actual being. (Both mouth and speech are used for communication with "others" outside of self.) The world and the created beings (the "others") make

it possible for there to be a divine kingdom, since "there cannot be a king without a nation," i.e., G-d cannot be a ruler without the existence of the element of "other."

In this sense, *malchut* is a passive *sefirah* that only contains that which the other *sefirot* pour into it. Paradoxically, however, it is specifically through *malchut* that the original creative plan is actualized. *Malchut* serves as a bridge between *Atzilut* and the lower worlds of *Beriah*, *Yetzirah*, and *Asiyah*, transmitting to them the G-dly life force that enlivens them. *Malchut* is thus considered the "source of life" for all the created beings of the lower worlds. So although *malchut* is actually lower than the previous six emotions, it is specifically through *malchut* that creation comes into being, thereby fulfilling G-d's desire for a dwelling place in the lower realms.

This is because the root and source of *malchut* is loftier than the other *sefirot*. Whereas the other *sefirot* are rooted in *keter*, *malchut* is rooted in the deepest and innermost level of the Essence of G-d which is utterly beyond the realm of knowledge. This realm is

ה.

אַךְ הִנֵּה הַנָּשִׁים לֹא רָצוּ בָּזֶה וְלָכֵן לֹא הִשְׁתַּתְּפוּ עִמָּהֶם
וְלֹא נָתְנוּ נִזְמֵיהֶם לַעֲשׂוֹת הָעֵגֶל,

וְהוּא מִצַּד שֹׁרֶשׁ נִשְׁמוֹתֵיהֶם שֶׁהוּא עִנְיָן הֱיוֹתָם מֵעָלְמָא
דְנוּקְבָא, אֲשֶׁר מַלְכוּתוֹ בַּכֹּל מָשָׁלָה׳׳, בְּחִינַת מַלְכוּת רֹאשׁ
עַל כָּל הָע׳ שָׂרִים שֶׁלְּמַעְלָה, וְיָדְעוּ וְהִרְגִּישׁוּ בְּנַפְשׁוֹתָם אֵיךְ
שֶׁאֵין מַמָּשׁ בִּמְזָלוֹת וְשָׂרִים הַנַּ׳׳ל יוֹתֵר מֵאֲשֶׁר יָדְעוּ
וְהִרְגִּישׁוּ הָאֲנָשִׁים, שֶׁנִּשְׁמוֹתֵיהֶם מֵעָלְמָא דְדְכוּרָא, בְּחִינַת

called *radla*, an acronym for *reisha d'lo ityada*, "the unknown beginning."

An analogy for this is found in *Yom Tov Shel Rosh Hashanah, 5659* (Kehot, 2000), p. 28ff., and particulary, p. 33: The root of speech surpasses that of emotions. When one speaks words of love, this arouses even greater love than before, because speech is rooted in the essence of the soul, conforming to the rule, "the end is wedged in the beginning, and the beginning is wedged in the end" (*Sefer Yetzirah* 1:7).

This is similar to the fact that although the woman is a recipient from the man, it is specifically through the woman that the man can procreate. See *The Majestic Bride* (Kehot, 2008), p. 26: "In the Torah's account of the creation of man and woman, it is only after *male and female He created them* that *G-d blessed them* (Genesis 1:27-28). Man alone was unworthy of G-d's blessing; it was only after G-d created the woman that He blessed them both, and said to them, *Be fruitful and multiply....* The reason for this is because the 'transmitter' (man) cannot realize his purpose (*Be fruitful and multiply...*) without a 'recipient' (woman)."

And because the souls of women are rooted in *malchut*, they are generally more predisposed to being sensitive to the presence of G-dliness as it dwells within these lower realms, as the discourse proceeds to explain. See below, fn. 116, for the comparison of women to *malchut*.

103. Psalms 103:19.

104. The seventy ministering angels are nullified in relation to *malchut*. *Malchut* spreads its rule over all the levels lower than it, down to govern the laws of nature in this lowly world. This is evident from the following verses: Psalms 145:13; Proverbs 29:4; Genesis 18:25; Psalms 45:9; Jeremiah 10:7. (*Or Hatorah, Nach*, vol. 2, p. 927; *Maamarei Admur Hazaken, Inyanim*, ibid.).

105. Z'EYR ANPIN. Literally "small face," this is the Kabbalistic term used collectively for the six *middot* or *sefirot* of *chesed, gevurah, tiferet, netzach, hod,* and *yesod*. It is often abbreviated as *z'a*.

106. ATZILUT. *Atzilut* is the loftiest of

exalted and elevated above and beyond the worlds of *Beriah*, *Yetzirah* and *Asiyah*.[107]

For this reason, those who deny [G-d's] detailed supervision say, *His glory transcends the heavens*[45]—[the "heavens" here representing] *z'a* of *Atzilut*—and He *has abandoned the earth*[26]—[the "earth" representing] *malchut*.[108]

Therefore, [the idolaters] establish their calendars according to the sun[109] rather than the moon for this same reason: Notwithstanding the fact that the sun is indeed superior to the moon,[110] yet this is precisely the point: the error lies in saying that *His glory transcends the heavens*, [that His glory is] upon the spiritual realm, with no role in the physical realm at all.[111]

By contrast, the Jews establish their calendar according to the moon, as if to declare that He is both G-d of the earth

---

the four worlds described above in fn. 32. It is a G-dly world (*Tanya*, Ch. 49). In *Atzilut*, there is no feeling of self or being, just an awareness of something higher, something beyond—G-dliness. *Atzilut* is therefore not considered to be a *created* world, but rather an *emanated* world. It is in *Atzilut* that G-d's attributes (the ten *sefirot*) are first manifest. For more on *Atzilut*, see *Mystical Concepts in Chassidism*, Ch. 4, and *The Four Worlds* (Kehot, 2003), pp. 24-28.

Regarding the men's souls and the masculine plane, see above, fn. 101.

107. See *Or Hatorah, Tissa*, p. 1987.

In *Maamarei Admur Hazaken, Inyanim*, p. 386: "The attributes of *Atzilut* are called *Havaya*, which is exalted and loftier than *sovev kol almin*, beyond even serving as a source for *Beriah, Yezirah*, and *Asiyah*, as implied by the verse (Psalms 148:13), *Let them praise the name of the L-rd, for His name is sublime, to Himself.*

This level, *Havaya*, was not even revealed to the Patriarchs, as it is written (Exodus 6:3), *I did not allow them to know Me by My name Havaya.*"

In a transcriber's notes of the discourse: "From *z'a*, which is beyond *Beriah, Yezirah*, and *Asiyah*, it is impossible for there to emerge a revelation that will be sensed by the human soul. *Malchut*, from where such a revelation can emerge, does not serve as the root of the men. So how would they have ever sensed that the constellations bare no substance? They therefore mistakenly followed the mixed multitude."

108. See *Zohar, Tosefta Bereshit*, 31b.

In *Maamarei Admur Hazaken, Inyanim*, p. 386: "*Malchut* is called 'earth,' as in the verse (Isaiah 66:1), *The earth is My footstool*. The nations maintain that *His glory transcends the heavens*, i.e., the 'glory of G-d' refers to the realm of *sovev kol almin*, exalted and lofty, termed [elsewhere] 'the glo-

זו"א דַאֲצִילוּת שֶׁמְרוֹמָם וְנִשְׂגָּב לְמַעְלָה מַעְלָה מֵעֵרֶךְ בִּי"עַ"
לְגַמְרֵי,

אֲשֶׁר עַל כֵּן אוֹמְרִים הַמַּכְחִישִׁים בְּהַשְׁגָּחָה פְּרָטִיּוּת, שֶׁעַל
הַשָּׁמַיִם כְּבוֹדוֹ שֶׁל מָקוֹם הוּא בְּחִינַת זו"א דַאֲצִילוּת, וְעָזַב
אֶת הָאָרֶץ הַיְינוּ בְּחִינַת מַלְכוּתיי,

וְלָכֵן הֵם מוֹנִים לַחַמָּהיט וְלֹא לַלְּבָנָה מִטַּעַם הַנ"ל, וְעִם
הֱיוֹת כִּי הַחַמָּה הִיא לְמַעְלָה בְּמַדְרֵגָה מֵהַלְּבָנָה, הִיא
הַנוֹתֶנֶת, שֶׁבְּזֶה שֶׁבְּזֶה עַצְמוֹ הוּא טָעוּתָם בְּאָמְרָם שֶׁעַל הַשָּׁמַיִם
כְּבוֹדוֹ בִּבְחִינַת הָרוּחָנִיּוּת וְאֵין לוֹ חֵלֶק בְּגַשְׁמִיּוּת כְּלָל כו',

וְיִשְׂרָאֵל הַמוֹנִים לַלְּבָנָה כְּלוֹמַר לִהְיוֹתוֹ אֱלֹקֵי הָאָרֶץ
כְּמוֹ אֱלֹקֵי הַשָּׁמַיִם, מַעְלָה וּמַטָּה שָׁוִים לְפָנָיו יִתְבָּרֵךְ, שֶׁעָם

---

ry of the Omnipresent,' which is *z'a,* and refers to the realm of 'space,' as it is written (Exodus 33:21), *I have a special place,* and (Hosea 5:15) *I will depart and return to My place,* and (Ezekiel 3:12) *From His place. He has abandoned the earth,* i.e., *malchut,* so that the ministering angels will be in charge, as it is written, *The heavens are the L-rd's heavens.* Hence, the men believed in the management of the ministering angels and the constellations."

109. *Sukkah* 29a.

110. The *Zohar* (I:249b, 251b) compares *malchut* to "the moon that has no light of its own save that which is given to it from the sun." Additionally, *Eitz Chaim* (6:5, 8:5, et passim) speaks of *malchut* as being "a dim speculum, because it has no (light) of its own."

111. I.e., the fact that the idolaters give central importance to the role of the sun, rather than the moon, is consistent with their attitude that G-d is lofty and remote.

In *Maamarei Admur Hazaken, Inyanim,* p. 386: "They mistakenly claim that...no energy descended from G-d for the physical realm at all. Thus, all the days of the year depend specifically on spirituality, as it is written (Genesis 8:22), *As long as the earth lasts,* and similarly (Job 8:9), *Our days on earth are like a shadow,* as it is written (Psalms 139:16), *Even those [happenings] to be formed in future days—to Him they are the same,* and this is called (cf. Deuteronomy 11:21) *as long as the heavens are above the earth.* They therefore establish their calendars according to the sun, which is high up in the heavens specifically—and do not establish their calendars according to the moon, which represents *malchut* and is called *G-d of the earth* specifically [see fn. 112]—for they maintain that He *has abandoned the earth,* as discussed above."

and G-d of the heavens,[112] and that above and below are equal before Him.[113] Thus, although the earth is subordinate to the heavens, *[G-d] looks down so low*—with detailed supervision—*upon heaven and earth*[46] equally. Indeed, [precisely because] G-d *dwells on high*[46] does He *look down so low upon heaven and earth* equally, for in truth, even the heavens are a descent and degradation for Him.[114]

Women are rooted specifically in *malchut*, and thus are similar to the moon,[115] which waxes and wanes every month like their feminine cycle,[116] as every thirty days they become impure and are then sanctified.[117] Consequently, they did not

---

112. Cf. Genesis 24:3, 7, and *Rashi* there.

113. In *Maamarei Admur Hazaken, Inyanim,* pp. 386-7: "The Jews establish their calendar according to the moon specifically, for 'there is no constellation for the Jews' [see fn. 48], and *The L-rd is G-d* (Deuteronomy 4:35) for the Jewish people on earth specifically, as explained above. Although to rule upon a lowly world constitutes a lower level of dominion, and the truth is that His name is sublime, to Himself, yet this is precisely the point: G-d's infinite light is loftier and more exalted than the level it is perceived to be by the idolaters, who call Him the 'G-d of gods.' His rule and supervision on such a low plane is precisely because He is so tremendously exalted. For 'Whatever is more exalted, can descend lower.'

"...In comparison to G-d's Essence, 'above' and 'below' are synonymous, and so He rules over both in an equal manner, as it is written (Jeremiah 23:24), *I fill the heavens and the earth*—equally, and (I Chronicles 29:11) *All that is in the heavens and on earth*, which *Targum* translates as 'that is *unified* in the heavens and the earth.' This is comparable to a circle, which has no higher or lower part.... This also conforms to the opinion that the heavens and the earth were created simultaneously, as stated elsewhere [*Chagigah* 12a]."

114. Cf. Job 15:15. Because G-d is so incomparably superior (i.e., "enthroned on high") to both the spiritual and the physical realms, His involvement in even the loftiest of spiritual realms constitutes a descent for Him. See *Tanya*, Ch. 48, which explains this concept in terms of the comparative values of the numbers 1 and 1 million in their relative value to infinity.

In a transcriber's notes of the discourse: "This verse [*Who is like the L-rd our G-d Who dwells on High [yet] looks down so low upon heaven and earth*] is in response to the prior verse. First it states, *The L-rd is high above the nations*, which refers to the opinion that *G-d has abandoned the world*. To this the verse provides a response: On the contrary, because *[G-d dwells] on high*, He *[looks] down so low upon*

הֱיוֹת שֶׁהָאָרֶץ הִיא לְמַטָּה בְּמַדְרֵגָה מִשָּׁמַיִם מִכָּל מָקוֹם הִנֵּה
הוּא מַשְׁפִּילִי לִרְאוֹת בְּהַשְׁגָּחָה פְּרָטִיּוּת בַּשָּׁמַיִם וּבָאָרֶץ בְּשָׁוֶה
מַמָּשׁ, וְהַיְינוּ מִפְּנֵי הֱיוֹתוֹ מַגְבִּיהִי לָשָׁבֶת, שֶׁלָּכֵן הוּא
מַשְׁפִּילִי לִרְאוֹת בַּשָּׁמַיִם וּבָאָרֶץ בְּשָׁוֶה כו׳, כִּי בֶּאֱמֶת גַּם
הַשָּׁמַיִם הֵם בְּחִינַת יְרִידָה וְהַשְׁפָּלָה לְפָנָיו,

אַךְ הִנֵּה הַנָּשִׁים לְפִי שֶׁשָּׁרְשָׁם מִבְּחִינַת הַמַּלְכוּת דַּוְקָא,
וְלָכֵן כְּמוֹ שֶׁבַּלְּבָנָה יֵשׁ מִיעוּט וְרִיבּוּי בְּכָל חֹדֶשׁ, כֵּן הוּא
עוֹנַת הַנָּשִׁים° בְּוִסְתָּן מִשְׁלֹשִׁים יוֹם לִשְׁלֹשִׁים יוֹם

---

heaven and earth equally—to negate that opinion."

115. In *Maamarei Admur Hazaken, Inyanim*, p. 387: "Similar to the moon receiving from the sun, the woman receives from the man. The sun and moon are called male and female, and the moon has nothing of its own, save for what it receives from the sun. A woman too, can only procreate when she receives from a man." See also the Tzemach Tedek's commentary on Psalms, *Yahel Or*, p. 401, sect. 6.

116. See *Or Hatorah, Tissa*, p. 1987, where reference is made to: *Darkei Moshe, Orach Chaim* #417, quoting *Or Zarua*; *Zohar* I:64a; *Sefer Chasidim* #1148; *Pri Eitz Chaim, Shaar Rosh Chodesh*, Ch. 3.

117. The three concepts of *malchut*, the moon, and the women, are comparable, albeit as manifest on different levels of creation:

Malchut: As noted above in fn. 101, *malchut* is, paradoxically, a passive *sefirah* that only contains that which the other *sefirot* pour into it, and is also the bridge between *Atzilut*

and the lower worlds, transmitting to them the G-dly life force that enlivens them, actualizing G-d's original creative plan. There are different times when each of these functions is active: Sometimes *malchut* receives the flow and internalizes it, while at others, *malchut* lowers itself to sustain the lower worlds. (See *True Existence*, (Kehot, 2002), fn. 65; *The Majestic Bride* (Kehot, 2008), fn. 95).

Moon: During the first half of the month, the moon increasingly reflects the sun's light until it is "full," after which, it begins to gradually diminish. After having become completely "dark," it reappears and is sanctified, signifying the beginning of a new month—*Rosh Chodesh*.

Women: The female, the source from which life actually emerges, receives the flow provided by the male. On her own, however, she would not be able to procreate. The womb first develops (to become hospitable for fertilization), and then, after its peak, turns to empty itself. When that stage is completed (i.e., after the cessation of flow), the woman immerses in a *mikveh* and is sanctified again.

accede to the mixed multitude regarding the calf, unlike the men, who are from the masculine plane [and so did not reject the mixed multitude].

For this reason, the holiday of *Rosh Chodesh*, which is the holiday of the moon and time of its ascent,[118] was given more to women than to men.[119] And although women are generally exempt from all time-bound positive commands, [the observance of] *Rosh Chodesh* does not fall into this category, since their souls [like the moon] are rooted in the feminine plane.[120]

118. The term "ascent" is not used in the common astrological usage, but rather, in describing the moon's separation from its conjunction with the sun as it begins its waxing phase.

119. Women share a special bond with the moon as both are spiritually rooted in and embody the quality of

malchut, as explained in fn. 116. It is this relationship to *malchut* that makes women more inclined to reject the fundamental error of a reasoning that leads to idolatry. Accordingly, we now understand the relevance of what was mentioned at the beginning of this discourse that women were granted *Rosh Chodesh* specifically as a re-

שֶׁטְמֵאָה וּמִתְקַדֶּשֶׁת, וְלָכֵן הֵם לֹא קִיבְּלוּ מֵהָעֶרֶב רַב בְּעִנְיַן הָעֵגֶל כַּאֲשֶׁר קִיבְּלוּ הָאֲנָשִׁים שֶׁהֵם מֵעָלְמָא דִּדְכוּרָא,

וְלָכֵן בְּיוֹם טוֹבֵסיא שֶׁל רֹאשׁ חֹדֶשׁ שֶׁהוּא יוֹם טוֹב שֶׁל הַלְּבָנָה וְעֵת הִתְעַלּוּתָהּ כו׳ נִיתַּן לְנָשִׁים יוֹתֵר מֵאֲנָשִׁים מִטַּעַם הַנַּ״ל, וַהֲגַם כִּי בְּכָל מִצְוַת עֲשֵׂה שֶׁהַזְּמַן גְּרָמָא הַנָּשִׁים פְּטוּרוֹת, מִכָּל מָקוֹם רֹאשׁ חֹדֶשׁ אֵינוֹ דוֹמֶה לָזֶה, לִהְיוֹת כִּי שָׁרְשָׁם הוּא בְּעָלְמָא דְּנוּקְבָּא כו׳.

———◆›⊙‹◆———

---

ward for their wholesale refusal to take part in the sin of the Golden Calf. See also *Maamarei Admur Hazaken, Inyanim*, p. 387.

120. Although we might reason that women should be exempt from celebrating *Rosh Chodesh* based on *halachic* axioms, the truth is the op-posite. *Rosh Chodesh* is uniquely relevant to women, for it bears witness to the characteristically feminine spiritual view that G-d is immanently present in this world and does not separate Himself from its management through independent intermediaries.

HEBREW NOTES

הערות לד"ה להבין ענין ראש חדש

א) להבין ענין ר"ח: בספר התולדות של כ"ק אדמו"ר מהר"ש קה"ת תש"ז – ברשימת מאמרי שנה זו – ע' 51 אודות מאמר זה כותב כ"ק אדמו"ר: "יו"ט של נשים כו' חטא העגל כו' טעות פרעה עזב ה'".

למאמר זה ראה מאמרי אדה"ז על ענינים ע' שפג ואילך. ונו"א שם ע' שפד ואילך. אוה"ת תשא ע' א'תתקפה ואילך.

בסה"מ תר"ם בחלק ההנחות נדפסה הנחה ממאמר זה ושם הפתיחה: מי כה"א המגביהי לשבת.

באג"ק כ"ק אדמו"ר מהר"ש ע' כא מאור ליו' ב' ה' תשרי תר"ם כותב: חושב אני לשבות אי"ה פ' נח בפאריז, כי לפי החשבון נבוא אי"ה צלחה שעה 9.45 יום וש"ק בקר לפאריז, ומשם הוא 18 שעות למאנטרע. אמנם ממאמר זה וכן ממאמר הבא ד"ה ואעשך לגוי גדול משמע שעדיין הי' בליובאוויטש. ראה גם מאמר ד"ה כמגדל דוד צוארך תר"ם ובהערה 1.

ב) ר"ח . . כלליות החיות: ראה שפע טל ש"ח, פ"ג (טל קמא, סע"ב). לקו"ת ר"ה נח, א. מאמרי אדה"ז תקס"ז נ' נג. עט"ר ג, ב. אוה"ת קרח ע' תרפט.

ג) ראש השנה . . כלליות חיות: ראה לקו"ת תבא מא, ג. ר"ה נג, ד. נח, א. עט"ר שם.

ד) ר"ח הוא יו"ט של נשים: ראה ירושלמי פסחים רפ"ד. פדר"א פמ"ה וברד"ל שם. רש"י מגילה כב, ב ד"ה ראשי חדשים. אוה"ת חנוכה כרך ה' ע' 1864 (הובא גם בסה"מ תר"ם ח"ב (בחלק המאמרים) מאמר ד"ה רני ושמחי על יד הערה 52 ואילך). לקו"ש ר"ח תמוז כרך ח ע' 315 הערה 8.

ה) יותר מהאנשים: ראה גם לקו"ת ברכה צז, סע"ג ואילך. אוה"ת בראשית ע' כד. רד"ק לשמואל-א כ, כז, יט. לקו"ת וארא כרך ג ע' 862 הערה 49. לקמן בהנחה כאן.

ו) שהנשים פטורי' ממ"ע שהזמ"ג: קדושין כט, א במשנה. ראה גם סה"מ תרל"ח ע' קנח ואילך. וש"נ.

ז) במשנה . . ע"פ חשבון: ראה ר"ה פ"ב, מ"ו ואילך.

ח) עכשיו . . ע"פ חשבון: ראה גם לקו"ש בא כרך טז ע' 94 הערה 10.

ט) כי בשש משה: תשא לב, א (וברש"י שם). שבת פט, א.

י) אלה אלקיך ישראל: תשא שם, ד. ח.

יא) דור דיעה: ראה זהר בשלח סב, ב. פע"ח שחה"מ שכ"א, פ"א. מאמרי אדה"א דברים ח"א ע' עו. וש"נ. סה"מ תר"ם ח"ב (בחלק המאמרים) מאמר ד"ה והנה כובע על יד הערה *109: הצד"ג.

יב) טעותם ויום המעונן: ראה רש"י תשא ושבת שם.

יג) טעות פרעה: ראה ספר הערכים חב"ד כרך ב מערכת אוה"ע ע' רעז ואילך.

יד) מי הוי' . . את הוי': שמות ה, ב.

טו) כי ממזרח שמש עד מבואו: מלאכי א, יא [ושם: ועד – אבל כ"ה גם באוה"ת כאן].

טז) דקרו לי' אלקא דאלקייא: מנחות בסופה. ראה סה"מ תרל"ב ח"א ע' נג בהערה.

יז) הודו לאלקי האלקים: תהלים קלו, ב.

יח*) שהוא: אוצ"ל: הוא.

יח) עזב ה' את הארץ: יחזקאל ח, יב. ט.

יט)   השמים שמים להוי': תהלים קטו, טז.

כ)   שמים לרום: משלי כה, ג.

כא)   כגבוה שמים מארץ: תהלים קג, יא.

כב)   שבארץ יון . . אלקות: ראה גם מאמרי אדה"ז על ענינים כאן ע' שפג. סה"מ
תר"ם (בחלק ההנחות) בהנחה כאן.

כד)   המושל המושל: כ"ה בהכת"י.

כג)   כל השפעה . . המושל ושולט: ראה אגה"ק סכ"ה (קלט, ב). שע"ת ו, א ובהערה
3. מאמרי אדה"א דברים ח"א ע' קסד. וש"נ.

כה)   על השמים . . כבודו: תהלים קיג, ד.

כו)   והמגביהי לשבת . . משפילי לראות: תהלים קיג, ה. ו. ראה גם לקמן בסיום
המאמר. סידור שער תפלת ר"ה רלז, ג. מאמרי אדה"א דברים ח"ג ריש ע' א'לה. תו"ח
ויחי רמד, סע"ד, ואילך.

כז)   מאמינים בני מאמינים: שבת צז, א. וראה אוה"ת בראשית כרך ג ע' 1104 תשא
ע' א'תתעט.

כח)   שאין מזל לישראל: שבת קנו, א. ראה מאמרי אדה"א שמות ח"ב ע' שפ. וש"נ.

כט)   למען תדע שאין . . הארץ: וארא ט, יד [ושם: כי אין].

ל)   למען ספר . . הארץ: וארא שם, טז [ושם: ולמען].

לא)   וידעת היום: ואתחנן ד, לט. ראה גם סה"מ תר"ם מאמר ד"ה סמוכים לעד
ספ"ב.

לב)   פרעה . . מש' אלקים ידע: ראה תו"א מקץ מג, רע"א. סידור שער החנוכה
ערא, סע"ב.

לג)   אלקים הוא לשון כח: ראה שו"ע אדה"ז דין כוונת הברכות ס"ה, ס"ג. תו"ח
וארא ח"א עה, ב. וש"נ.

לד)   ואת אילי הארץ: יחזקאל יז, יג.

לה)   אלקים . . שלום פרעה: מקץ מא, טז.

לו)   שהוא הנותן לך כח לעשות חיל: עקב ח, יח.

לז)   על כל דרכי . . מעלליו: ירמי' לב, יט.

לח)   כגרזן ביד החוצב: מו"נ ח"ג פכ"ט. זהר בראשית לו, א. ישעי' י, טו.

לט)   מט"ט שהוא שרו של עולם: ראה יבמות טז, ב ובתוס' שם. בסה"מ תר"ם מאמר
ד"ה כמגדל דוד צוארך על יד הערה 20. שם ח"ב (בחלק המאמרים) מאמר ד"ה רני
ושמחי (פיסקאות והנה פי' ולפי"ז) ובהנחת כ"ק אדמו"ר מהורש"ב שם על יד הערה 13.
מאמרי אדה"א ויקרא ח"ב ע' תתעא. במדבר ח"ב ע' תשצ. דברים ח"ג ע' תשצד.

מ)   אין אומן בלא כלים: בסה"מ תר"ם (בחלק ההנחות) בהנחה כאן בשם רז"ל —
ראה גבול בנימין לר' בנימין הכהן אמשטרדם תפ"ז ח"א בתחילתו: אמרו המושלים.
פמ"ג לאו"ח (בהקדמה) באגרת הראשונה.

מא)   האלקים ל' רבים: רש"י וירא כ, יג. וישלח לה, ז. ראה תו"א וארא נו, ב. תו"ח
שם ס, א ואילך. לקו"ת אמור לא, ג.

מב)   וא"ת מחוי' אלא מהוה: ראה שער היחוה"א פ"ב ובמ"מ, הגהות והע"ק שם.
הערה בסה"מ תש"ד ע' 20.

מד)   שבטבע הטוב להטיב: ראה עמק המלך שער שעשועי המלך בתחילתו. שומר
אמונים ויכוח שני סי"ד. שער היחוה"א פ"ד ובמ"מ הגהות והע"ק לשם. ולהעיר משו"ת
חכם צבי סי"ח.

מג)   וכמ"ש ובטובו מחדש . . התחדשות: ברכת יוצר. ראה גם הגהת כ"ק אדמו"ר

מהר"ש באוה"ת בראשית כרך ו ע' 2040 סה"מ תרל"ו ח"ב ס"ע רנא. תרע"ח ע' קכ. לקמן ע' תטז. וש"נ.

מה) אין עוד . . ענין השיתוף: ראה סה"מ תרכ"ט ע' קנה ואילך ובהנסמן שם. סה"מ מלוקט א' ע' נה.

מו) השמיע: כ"ה בהכת"י.

מז) שגם באלקיהם עשה שפטים: ראה מסעי לג, ד. בא יב, יב.

מח) י"ב מזלות ברקיע: ברכות לב, ב. רמב"ם הל' יסוה"ת פ"ג, ה"ו.

מט) ומזל מצרים . . טלה: ראה זהר פינחס רנ, ב. זח"א בהשמטות רנו, א (סכ"ב).

נ) הן נזבח . . לעיניהם: וארא ח, כב.

נא) שכל עיקר ענין מצות קרבן פסח: ראה זהר ורע"מ פינחס רנא, א ואילך.

נב) לשחוט שה: בא יב, ו.

נג) ועצם . . בו: בא שם, מו.

נד) ולא תאכלו: שם שם, ט [ושם: אל תאכלו].

נה) כי לא . . עם העברים: מקץ מג, לב [ושם: את – ראה גם מאמרי אדה"ז כאן]. ראה תרגום אונקלוס שם. וראה גם לקו"ש ויחי כרך ה ע' 266 שולי הגליון הב'.

נו) שהמזלות נלחמים . . בדניאל: ראה שם פ"י ואילך.

נו) מלכותו בכל משלה: ע"פ תהלים קג, יט.

נז) ז"א . . למעלה מעלה מערך בי"ע: ראה אוה"ת כאן ס"ע א'תתקפז ואילך.

נח) הארץ . . מל': ראה זהר תוספתא בראשית לא, ב.

נט) הם מונים לחמה: סוכה כט, א.

ס) שבלבנה . . עונת הנשים: ראה אוה"ת כאן ע' א'תתקפז.

סא) ביו"ט: אוצ"ל: יו"ט.

BIBLIOGRAPHY

BIBLIOGRAPHY

Ateret Rosh: Chasidic exposition of Rosh Hashanah, Yom Kippur, the Ten Days of Penintence and Shabbat Shuvah by R. DovBer, second Lubavitcher Rebbe. Kopust, 1821; Shanghai, 1947; Revised Edition, Brooklyn, NY, 1989. (Heb.)

Avodah Zarah: Talmudic tractate discussing the subject of idolatry.

Bava Batra: Talmudic tractate discussing certain monetary issues.

Bechorot: Talmudic tractate discussing the laws of the offerings of firstborn animals.

Berachot: Talmudic tractate discussing the laws of blessings.

Bereishit Rabbah: See *Midrash Rabbah*.

Chacham Tzvi (Responsa): Responsa by R. Tzvi Hirsch Ashkenazi (1656-1718). First published in Amsterdam, 1712.

Chullin: Talmudic tractate discussing various laws of kosher and sacrifices.

Darkei Moshe: Commentary on the Tur by Rabbi Moshe Isserles (known as Rama, 1520-1572), as well as on *Beit Yosef*, which is R. Yosef Karo's commentary on the *Tur* and the work underlying the *Shulchan Aruch*.

Eitz Chaim: A compilation of the Arizal's Kabbalistic teachings, by his primary disciple and exponent, Rabbi Chaim Vital (1543-1620).

Emek Hamelech: Commentary on the Zohar and the writings of the Arizal by one of his disciples, R. Naftali Hertz Bachrach of Frankfurt. Amsterdam, 1648. Revised edition, Jerusalem, 2003. (Heb.)

Esther Rabbah: See *Midrash Rabbah*.

Four Worlds, The: English translation of a letter by R. Yosef Yitzchak Schneersohn, sixth Lubavitcher Rebbe, explaining the mystical worlds of Atzilut, Beriah, Yetzirah, and Asiyah (Kehot, 2003).

Gevul Binyamin: Expositions on the Torah portions and the Haftarot, and for festivals, eulogies, weddings, and circumcisions, by Rabbi Binyamin Hakohen. Amsterdam, 1727.

Iggeret Hakodesh: Fourth part of *Tanya* by R. Schneur Zalman of Liadi; a selection of letters by dealing with such topics as charity, prayer, and the like.

Jerusalem Talmud: See *Talmud.*

Kiddushin: Talmudic tractate discussing the laws of marriage.

Levush: Compendium of all Jewish laws, and Kabbalah, masterly in style and composition by Rabbi Mordechai Yaffe of Prague and later Chief Rabbi Posen (15301612). Due to his name being Mordechai, he named his work *Levush* (lit., "Clothes") after the description of the royal robes in which Mordechai of Shushan was clothed by King Achashverosh. (Ten volumes; Heb.)

Likkut Dinei Uminhagei Rosh Chodesh: Compilation of laws and Chabad customs on the subject of Rosh Chodesh, by Rabbi Chaim Rapaport (Kehot, 1990).

Likkutei Sichot: Talks delivered and edited by the Lubavitcher Rebbe, Rabbi Menachem M. Schneerson. (Thirty-nine volumes, Heb. / Yid.).

Likkutei Torah: A collection of discourses elucidating major themes of Leviticus, Numbers, Deuteronomy, Song of Songs, Pesach, Shavuot, the High Holidays and Sukkot according to Chasidic philosophy. Delivered by the founder of Chabad Chasidus, R. Schneur Zalman of Liadi, they were published in 5608 (1848) by his grandson R. Menachem Mendel Schneersohn, third Lubavitcher Rebbe, the "Tzemach Tzedek." (Heb.)

Maamarei Amdur Ha'emtzaei: Chasidic discourses by R. DovBer, second Lubavitcher Rebbe. 19 vol., Brooklyn, NY, 1985-1992.

Maamarei Admur Hazaken: Chasidic Discourses by R. Schneur Zalman of Liadi. 24 vol., Brooklyn, NY, 1956-2006.

Majestic Bride, The: English translation of two discourses. The first, *Lecha Dodi, 5689*, was delivered by R. Yosef Yitzchak Schneersohn, sixth Lubavitcher Rebbe, on the occasion of the wedding of his daughter, Rebbetzin Chaya Mushka, to Rabbi Menachem M. Schneerson. The second, *Lecha Dodi, 5714*, was delivered by the Lubavitcher Rebbe, Rabbi Menachem M. Schneerson, in 1953. (Kehot, 2008)

Marei Mekomot, Hagahot, V'Heorot Ketzorot L'Shaar Hayichud v'haEmunah: Scholarly handwritten notes of the Lubavitcher Rebbe, R. Menachem M. Schneerson, on the second part of the Tanya, published posthumously by Kehot Publication Society, 1999-2000.

Megillah: Talmudic tractate discussing the laws of Purim and Esther. Also expounds the Book of Esther.

Menachot: Talmudic tractate discussing various sacrifices in the *Beit Hamikdash*.

Midrash Rabbah: A major collection of homilies and commentaries on the Torah, attributed to Rabbi Oshaya Rabbah (circa. 3rd century); some place it as a work of the early Gaonic period.

Mishneh Torah: See *Rambam*.

Moreh Nevuchim: "Guide for the Perplexed." One of the most important works on Jewish philosophy, by R. Moshe ben Maimon; Rambam (Maimonides).

Mystical Concepts in Chasidism: Guide to the intricate concepts of Jewish mysticism found in Chabad Chasidic philosophy. Authored by Rabbi J. Immanuel Schochet (Kehot, 1988). (Eng.)

Nedarim: Talmudic tractate discussing oaths.

Niddah: Talmudic tractate discussing the laws of family purity.

Or Hatorah: Chasidic discourses and commentary on the Torah, Prophets, Writings, Talmud, Prayer and miscellaneous topics by R. Menachem Mendel Schneersohn, third Lubavitcher Rebbe, the "Tzemach Tzedek"; forty-one volumes, Kehot. (Heb.)

Or Torah: A compilation of Chasidic teachings by R. DovBer, the Maggid of Mezritch, and leader of the second generation of Chasidism. Compiled by his students, this work provides unique insight into various concepts contained in Scripture, Talmud, and Kabbalah, through the Chasidic lens. First printed in Koretz, 5564 (1804). New, revised edition, Brooklyn, NY, 2006. (Heb.)

Overcoming Folly: A comprehensive treatise by R. Shalom DovBer Schneersohn, fifth Lubavitcher Rebbe. Written in the spirit and style of traditional ethical Torah teachings, it touches upon the various challenges one experiences when faced with the reality of material existence–obstacles that stand in the way of achieving true spiritual heights. Brooklyn, NY, 2006. (Hebrew: *Kuntres Umaayan*, Brooklyn, NY 1943.)

Pardes (Pardes Rimonim): Kabbalistic work by R. Moshe Cordovero (Ramak) of Safed (1522-1570), leader of a prominent Kabbalistic school in Safed.

Pesikta Rabbati: A small book on the Festivals, containing Aphorisms of Talmudic Sages arranged similar to *Midrash Rabbah* (q.v.).

Pirkei d'Rabbi Eliezer: A Midrash authored by the second century Mishnaic Sage, R. Eliezer ben Horkenus, also known as Rabbi Eliezer Hagadol ("the great"). "The earliest of all Tannaic treatises, revealed and famous in the era of our authoritative Rabbis and mystical Kabbalists, the *Rishonim*, who used and benefited from its light" (from the title page).

Pri Etz Chaim: A compilation of the Arizal's mystical rituals pertaining to Prayer, recorded by R. Chaim Vital and arranged in the present order by the Kabbalist R. Meir Popporos (1624-1662).

Pri Megadim: A threefold commentary by Rabbi Yosef ben Meir Teomim (1727-1793) on the *Orach Chaim* and *Yoreh Deah* sections of the *Shulchan Aruch*: *Mishbetzot Zahav* on R. David ben Shmuel's *Turei Zahav*, *Eshel Avraham* on R. Avraham Abele's *Magen Avraham*, and *Siftei Daat* on Rabbi Shabbetai Cohen's *Siftei Kohen* (Frankfort-on-the-Oder, 1753). (Heb.)

Ra'aya Mehemna: Partially extant Midrash by R. Shimon bar Yochai, included in a section of the *Zohar*. Explaining the 613 mitzvot, it contains mystical descriptions of the human body.

Rambam: Acronym for R. Moshe ben Maimon (1135-1204), also known as Maimonides. Author of the Mishneh Torah, a phenomenal redaction of the entire Talmud, he is regarded as one of Judaism's foremost Torah authorities.

Reshit Chochmah: Classic ethichal work by R. Eliyahu de Vidas, disciple of R. Moshe Cordovero; completed in 1575.

Rosh Hashanah: Talmudic tractate discussing the laws of the Rosh Hashanah festival and the Jewish calendar.

Sanhedrin: Talmudic tractate discussing court justice and/or the Supreme Court in ancient Israel, consisting of 71 members.

Sefer Chassidim: Highly inspiring ethical work, including a collection thoughts and principles of the Jewish faith by

Rabbi Yehudah Hachasid (1150-1217). It also discusses the importance of sincere prayer, honesty and sincerity in one's personal relations to G-d and man, philosophical themes such as reward, punishment and Divine justice, along with laws for daily living. Often makes use of stories for illustration, and records many customs and beliefs.

Sefer Ha'arachim: Encyclopedia of a number of topics discussed in Chasidus, gathered from the writings of seven generations of Chabad Rebbes (Kehot).

Sefer Hachakirah: Also known as *Derech Emunah*, this work is a discussion on the creation of the world according to philosophy, Kabbalah and Chasidus, by R. Menachem Mendel of Lubavitch, the "Tzemach Tzedek."

Sefer Hamaamarim 5643-5680: Set of Chasidic discourses delivered by R. Shalom DovBer Schneersohn, fifth Lubavitcher Rebbe, between 5643-5680 (1883-1920), the years of his leadership; twenty-five volumes. (Heb.)

Sefer Hamaamarim Melukat: Chasidic discourses delivered and edited by the Lubavitcher Rebbe, Rabbi Menachem M. Schneerson, during the course of his leadership 5711-5752 (1951-1992). Six volumes (Kehot, 1987-1992). (Heb.)

Sefer Yetzirah: One of the oldest written sources of Kabbalah, it is attributed to the Patriarch Abraham. It has been the subject of over one hundred commentaries since it was first published in Mantua, 1562.

Shaar Hayichud v'haEmunah: Second part of Tanya; explores the doctrines of Divine Unity, Providence and faith; twelve chapters.

Shaarei Teshuvah: Chasidic work by R. DovBer, second Lubavitcher Rebbe in two parts. The first contains expositions of *teshuvah* (repentance), *bechirah* (free choice), and *tefillah* (prayer); the second part includes a distinct "*gate of teshuvah*" and a short work entitled *Chinuch*, (introductory Jewish education). Shklov, 1817-18; Shanghai, 1947; Revised Edition, Brooklyn, NY, 1995. (Heb.)

Shabbat: Talmudic tractate discussing the laws of Shabbat.

Shaloh: A monumental work by R. Yeshayah Horowitz, (1558-1628), chief rabbi of Prague. Also known by its acronym, *Shelah*, it contains explanations and commentaries on the profound aspects of the Torah, *mitzvot*, the festivals, Jewish customs and the fundamental beliefs of Judaism, including basic instruction in Kabbalah. First published in Amsterdam, 1648.

Shefa Tal: Kabbalistic work by R. Shabbetai Sheftel Horowitz of Prague (c. 1561-1619), to explain R. Aharon Hazaken's *Iggeret Hataamim*. First published in Hanau, 1612.

Shemot Rabbah: See *Midrash Rabbah*.

Shomer Emunim: A work confirming the truth of the Kabbalah, by R. Yosef Irgas (1685-1730), designed in debate form, between "Shaltiel" who emphasizes studying the Revealed Torah and "Yehoyada" who emphasizes studying Kabbalah. Amsterdam, 1736.

Shulchan Aruch Harav: Code of Jewish law by R. Schneur Zalman of Liadi. Shklov, 1814; Brooklyn, NY, 1960-8; 1999-2007.

Siddur im Dach: Lit., "Siddur with Chasidus." Also known as *Seder Tefillot Mikol Hashanah* (The Order of the Prayers of the Entire Year). Prayer book containing rulings and Chasidic discourses pertaining to the prayers by Rabbi Schneur Zalman of Liadi. (Heb.)

Siddur Tehillat Hashem, Annotated Edition: Newly set prayer book with detailed annotations in English. Includes illustrations, laws, and instructions. Brooklyn, NY, 2002.

Sukkah: Talmudic tractate discussing the festival of Sukkot and its laws.

Talmud: The embodiment of the Oral Law. Following the codification of the Mishnah by R. Yehudah Hanassi, c. 150 C.E., later discussions, known as the Talmud, were redacted in two parts. The more popular Babylonian Talmud was compiled by Rav Ashi and Ravina (about the end of the fifth century, C.E.). The Jerusalem Talmud was compiled by Rabbi Yochanan bar Nappacha (about the end of the third century, C.E.).

Tanchuma: Early Midrash on the Torah, attributed to R. Tanchuma bar Abba. Constantinople, 1522.

Tanya: Philosophical *magnum opus* by Rabbi Schneur Zalman of Liadi, in which the principles of Chabad are expounded. The name is derived from the initial word of this work. Also called *Likkutei Amarim.*

Tikkunei Zohar: A work of seventy chapters on the first word of the Torah, by the school of R. Shimon bar Yochai (circa. 120 C.E.). First printed in Mantua, 1558, *Tikkunei Zohar* contains some of the most important discussions in *Kabbalah*, and is essential for understanding the *Zohar*.

Torah Or: A collection of discourses elucidating major themes of the weekly Torah portion and Festivals according to Chassidic philosophy. Delivered by the founder of Chabad Chasidus, R. Schneur Zalman of Liadi (1745-1812), they were published by his grandson R. Menachem Mendel of Lubavitch, the Tzemach Tzedek (1789-1866).

Torat Chaim: A collection of discourses elucidating major themes of the Torah portions of Bereishit-Pekudei, by R. DovBer of Lubavitch. Kopust, 1886; Brooklyn NY, 1974; 2003.

Torat Shmuel 5626-5640: Set of Chasidic discourses delivered by R. Shmuel Schneersohn, fourth Lubavitcher Rebbe, between 5626-5640 (1866-1880), the years of his leadership [5626-5643 (1866-1882)]; twenty-three volumes. (Heb.)

True Existence: English translation of *Mi Chamocha, 5629,* delivered by R. Shmuel Schneersohn, fourth Lubavitcher Rebbe, on Shabbat *Yitro* and Shabbat *Shemini* 5629 (1869). (Kehot, 2002)

Yahel Or: Chasidic discourses and commentary on Psalms by R. Menachem Mendel Schneersohn, third Lubavitcher Rebbe, the "Tzemach Tzedek." Poltava, 1918; Brooklyn, NY, 1953; 1984. (Heb.)

Yevamot: Talmudic tractate discussing levirate marriage.

Yom Tov Shel Rosh Hashanah 5666: Series of discourses delivered by R. Shalom DovBer Schneersohn, fifth Lubavitcher Rebbe, during the years 5666-7 (1905-7), named for its opening words.

Zohar: Lit., "Radiance," this basic work of Kabbalah was compiled by R. Shimon Bar Yochai (second century Mishnaic sage) as a commentary on the Torah. (Hebrew / Aramaic)

INDEX

INDEX

OTHER TITLES IN
THE CHASIDIC HERITAGE SERIES

Rabbi Schneur Zalman of Liadi

THE ETERNAL BOND *from Torah Or*
Translated by Rabbi Ari Sollish
This discourse explores the spiritual significance of *brit milah*, analyzing two dimensions in which our connection with G-d may be realized. For in truth, there are two forms of spiritual circumcision. Initially, man must "circumcise his heart," freeing himself to the best of his ability from his negative, physical drives; ultimately, though, it is G-d who truly liberates man from his material attachment.

∾ଡ଼∾ଡ଼∾ଡ଼

JOURNEY OF THE SOUL from *Torah Or*
Translated by Rabbi Ari Sollish
Drawing upon the parallel between Queen Esther's impassioned plea to King Ahasuerus for salvation and the soul's entreaty to G-d for help in its spiritual struggle, this discourse examines the root of the soul's exile, and the dynamics by which it lifts itself from the grip of materialism and ultimately finds a voice with which to express its G-dly yearnings. Includes a brief biography of the author.

∾ଡ଼∾ଡ଼∾ଡ଼

TRANSFORMING THE INNER SELF from *Likkutei Torah*
Translated by Rabbi Chaim Zev Citron
This discourse presents a modern-day perspective on the Biblical command to offer animal sacrifices. Rabbi Schneur Zalman teaches that each of us possesses certain character traits that can be seen as "animalistic," or materialistic, in nature, which can lead a person toward a life of material indulgence. Our charge, then, is to "sacrifice" and transform the animal within, to refine our animal traits and utilize them in our pursuit of spiritual perfection.

∾ଡ଼∾ଡ଼∾ଡ଼

Rabbi DovBer of Lubavitch

FLAMES from *Shaarei Orah*
Translated by Dr. Naftoli Loewenthal
This discourse focuses on the multiple images of the lamp, the oil, the wick and the different hues of the flame in order to express profound guidance in the Divine service of every individual. Although *Flames* is a Chanukah discourse, at the same time, it presents concepts that are of perennial significance. Includes the first English biography of the author ever published.

Rabbi Menachem Mendel of Lubavitch, the Tzemach Tzedek

THE MITZVAH TO LOVE YOUR FELLOW AS YOURSELF from *Derech Mitzvotecha*
Translated by Rabbis Nissan Mangel and Zalman I. Posner
The discourse discusses the Kabbalistic principle of the "collective soul of the world of *Tikkun*" and explores the essential unity of all souls. The discourse develops the idea that when we connect on a soul level, we can love our fellow as we love ourselves; for in truth, we are all one soul. Includes a brief biography of the author.

Rabbi Shmuel of Lubavitch

TRUE EXISTENCE
Mi Chamocha 5629
Translated by Rabbis Yosef Marcus and Avraham D. Vaisfiche
This discourse revolutionizes the age-old notion of Monotheism, i.e., that there is no other god besides Him. Culling from Talmudic and Midrashic sources, the discourse makes the case that not only is there no other god besides Him, there is nothing besides Him—literally. The only thing that truly exists is G-d. Includes a brief biography of the author.

◈◈◈

TRUE EXISTENCE *The Chasidic View of Reality*

A Video-CD with Rabbi Manis Friedman

Venture beyond science and Kabbalah and discover the world of Chasidism. This Video-CD takes the viewer step-by-step through the basic Chasidic and Kabbalistic view of creation and existence. In clear, lucid language, Rabbi Manis Friedman deciphers these esoteric concepts and demonstrates their modern-day applications.

৶৶৶

CHANNELING THE DIVINE

Itta B'Midrash Tillim

Edited by Rabbi Avraham D. Vaisfiche

The Bar Mitzvah, the day a Jewish boy turns thirteen, is a turning point in his life. He comes of age, becoming responsible for adherence to the *mitzvot* and fully accountable for his actions—and everyone celebrates. Chabad Chasidim mark this milestone by having the "Bar Mitzvah boy" publicly deliver a discourse, originally delivered by Rabbi Shalom DovBer Schneersohn, fifth Lubavitcher Rebbe, on the occasion of his Bar Mitzvah in 5634 (1873). Its main theme is the cosmic impact of performing the mitzvah of *tefillin*, and the special connection between this mitzvah and the age of Bar Mitzvah.

Rabbi Shalom DovBer of Lubavitch

YOM TOV SHEL ROSH HASHANAH 5659

Discourse One

Translated by Rabbis Yosef Marcus and Moshe Miller

The discourse explores the attribute of *malchut* and the power of speech while introducing some of the basic concepts of Chasidism and Kabbalah in a relatively easy to follow format. Despite its title and date of inception, the discourse is germane throughout the year. Includes a brief biography of the author.

৶৶৶

OVERCOMING FOLLY

Kuntres Umaayan Mibeit Hashem
Translated by Rabbi Zalman I. Posner

In this classis ethico-philosophical work, Rabbi Shalom DovBer weaves Chasidic doctrine, Kabbalah thoughts, Biblical and Talmudic texts and candid insights into human frailties into a document structured and systematic, yet informal and personal—a text for study and meditation.

కోకోకో

THE SIMPLE SERVANT

UMikneh Rav 5666
Translated by Rabbi Yosef Marcus

This discourse elaborates upon three types of personalities with distinct approaches to Divine service: 1) The child of G-d, naturally committed; 2) The loyal servant of G-d, motivated by his appreciation of G-d; 3) The simple servant of G-d, driven by his acceptance of the yoke of Heaven. His apathy makes serving G-d difficult. Yet he does his work consistently because he is reaching beyond himself—overcoming his own nature.

Rabbi Yosef Yitzchak of Lubavitch

THE PRINCIPLES OF EDUCATION AND GUIDANCE

Klalei Hachinuch Vehahadrachah
Translated by Rabbi Y. Eliezer Danzinger

The Principles of Education and Guidance is a compelling treatise that examines the art of educating. In this thought-provoking analysis, Rabbi Yosef Yitzchak teaches how to assess the potential of any pupil, how to objectively evaluate one's own strengths, and how to successfully use reward and punishment—methods that will help one become a more effective educator.

కోకోకో

THE FOUR WORLDS

Translated by Rabbis Yosef Marcus and Avraham D. Vaisfiche
Overview by Rabbi J. Immanuel Schochet

At the core of our identity is the desire to be one with our source, and to know the spiritual realities that give our physical life the transcendental importance of the Torah's imperatives. In this letter to a yearning Chasid, the Rebbe explains the mystical worlds of *Atzilut*, *Beriah*, *Yetzirah*, and *Asiyah*.

⋖⋖⋖

ONENESS IN CREATION

Kol Hamaarich B'Echad 5690
Translated by Rabbi Y. Eliezer Danzinger

Said by Rabbi Yosef Yitzchak at the close of his 1930 visit to Chicago, this discourse explores the concept of Divine Unity as expressed in the first verse of the *Shema*. The discourse maintains that it is a G-dly force that perpetually sustains all of creation. As such, G-d is one with creation. And it is our study of Torah and performance of the mitzvot that reveals this essential oneness.

⋖⋖⋖

CREATION AND REDEMPTION

Hachodesh 5700
Translated by Rabbi Yosef Marcus

Tishrei celebrates Creation, the birth of the world, indicative of the natural order. Nissan commemorates the miraculous Exodus from Egypt, or the supernatural. In human terms, when struggling with the obfuscation of the natural, the key is to recognize the dimension where the limitations of the natural order do not exist. In fact, the physical exists only so that we may demonstrate how it too exposes the Divine truth. And when we recognize this, we can realize the supernatural even within the natural.

⋖⋖⋖

THE MAJESTIC BRIDE

Lecha Dodi 5689 / 5714

Translated by Rabbis Ari Sollish and Avraham D. Vaisfiche

Customarily recited by a groom at the Kabbalat Panim reception, *Lecha Dodi* traces the Kabbalistic meaning of the order of the wedding ceremony, when first the guests welcome the groom, and then walk with the groom to welcome the bride, at which point the groom covers the bride's face with the veil. The discourse cites a number of examples and other situations where similar procedures occur, finally applying the reasoning to groom and bride to understand the Kabbalat Panim ceremony and the purpose of marriage.

Rabbi Menachem M. Schneerson,
the Lubavitcher Rebbe

ON THE ESSENCE OF CHASIDUS

Kuntres Inyana Shel Toras Hachasidus

This landmark discourse explores the contribution of Chasidus to a far deeper and expanded understanding of Torah. The Rebbe analyzes the relationship Chasidus has with Kabbalah, the various dimensions of the soul, the concept of Moshiach and the Divine attributes.

৵৹৵৹৵৹

GARMENTS OF THE SOUL

Vayishlach Yehoshua 5736

By Rabbi Menachem M. Schneerson, the Lubavitcher Rebbe

Translated by Rabbi Yosef Marcus

Often what is perceived in this world as secondary is in reality most sublime. What appears to be mundane and inconsequential is often most sacred and crucial. Thus, at their source, the garments of the human, both physical and spiritual, transcend the individual.

৵৹৵৹৵৹

THE UNBREAKABLE SOUL
Mayim Rabbim 5738
Translated by Rabbi Ari Sollish

No matter how much one may be inundated with materialism, the flame of the soul burns forever. A discourse that begins with an unequivocal declaration, it speaks to one who finds pleasure in the material world, yet struggles to find spirituality in his or her life.

৵৵৵

VICTORY OF LIGHT
Tanu Rabanan Mitzvat Ner Chanukah 5738
Translated by Rabbi Yosef Marcus

Even darkness has a purpose: to be transformed into light. This discourse explains how we can draw strength from the story of Chanukah for our battle with spiritual darkness, so that we, like the Macabees of old, may attain a *Victory of Light*.

৵৵৵

THE PATH TO SELFLESSNESS
Yehudah Atah 5738
Translated by Rabbi Shmuel Simpson

Beginning with the words *Yehuda Atah*, the discourse examines the blessing which Yaakov blessed his fourth son, Yehuda, as compared to the blessings he gave his first three sons, Reuven, Shimon and Levi. Yaakov's sons embody distinctive forms of divine service, which correspond to distinct sections of the prayers of Shema and the Amidah. Using these distinctions, the discourse further derives lessons about the bond between the individual Jewish soul and G-d.

৵৵৵

NURTURING FAITH

Kuntres Purim Kattan 5752

Translated by Rabbi Yosef Marcus

At its core, this discourse discusses the function of a *nassi*, a Jewish leader, who awakens within every single person the deepest part of the soul. Similar to Moses, the *nassi* inspires the person so that one's most basic faith in G-d leaves the realm of the abstract and becomes real. *Nurturing Faith* will cultivate your bond with the Rebbe's role as the Moses of our generation.

৵৵৵

There are many important manuscripts
that are ready to go to press, but are
waiting for a sponsor like you.

Please consider one of these opportunities
and make an everlasting contribution to
Jewish scholarship and Chasidic life.

For more information please contact:

The Chasidic Heritage Series
770 Eastern Parkway
Brooklyn, New York 11213
Tel: 718.774.4000
E-mail: info@kehot.com

COMING SOON!

LO TIHYEH MESHAKELAH 5712
By the Lubavitcher Rebbe, Rabbi Menachem M. Schneerson
Translated by Rabbi Zalman Abraham

৯৶৯৶৯৶

STAYING THE COURSE
A collection of discourses by the Chabad Rebbes on the eternal bond between Rebbe and Chasid that continues after the Rebbe's passing.

৯৶৯৶৯৶

PADAH BESHALOM 5668
By Rabbi Shalom DovBer of Lubavitch
Translated by Rabbi Zalman Abraham

לזכות

הרה"ת הרה"ח אי"א נו"נ עוסק בצרכי ציבור באמונה

ר' **מאיר אשר** שיחי'

גניביש

ליום הולדתו הארבעים לאורך ימים ושנים טובות
לשנת הצלחה וברכה בכל אשר יפנה

❀

נדפס ע"י
משפחתו שיחיו